THE
COMMUNITY

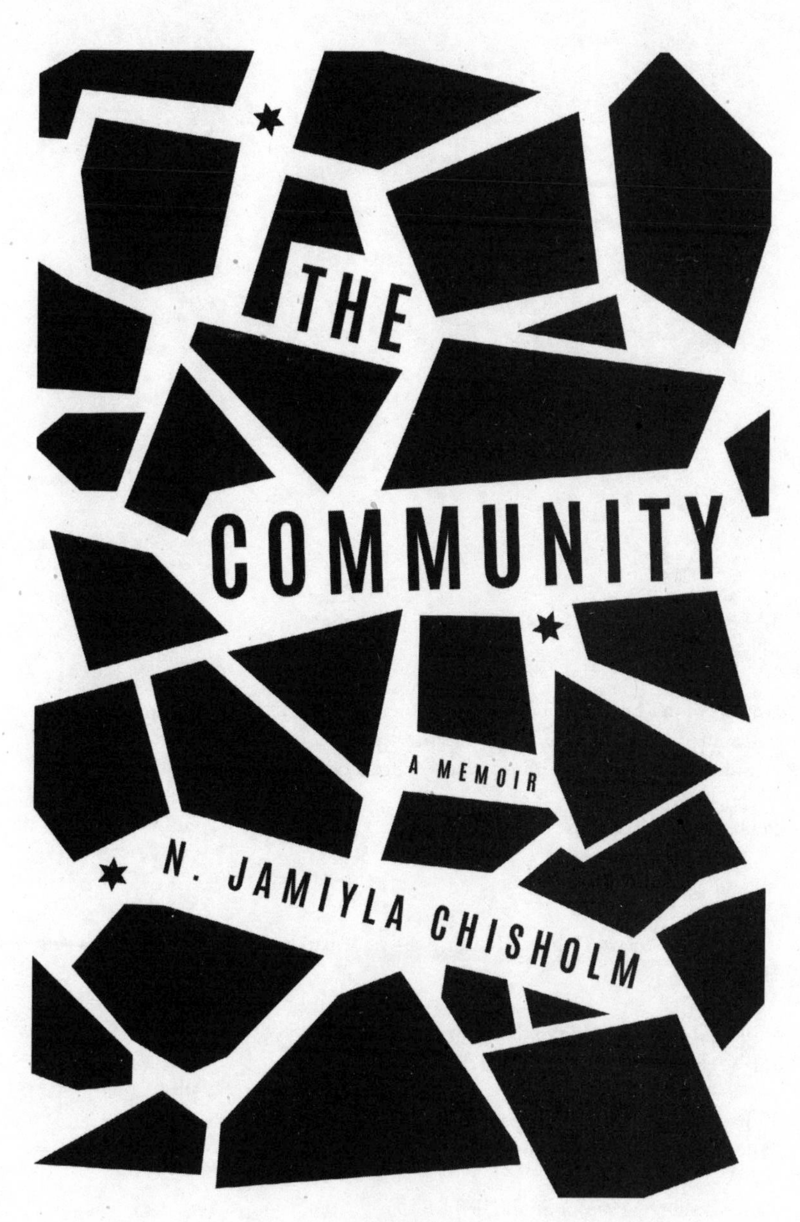

Little
a

Published by Little A, New York

www.apub.com

ISBN-13: 9781542037396 (hardcover)
ISBN-10: 1542037395 (hardcover)

ISBN-13: 9781542037389 (paperback)
ISBN-10: 1542037387 (paperback)

Cover design by Faceout Studio, Jeff Miller

Printed in the United States of America

First edition

For my mother, who helped me to remember, and to all the children who have been separated from their mothers, even for a brief moment, and refuse to forget.

Freedom is never voluntarily given by the oppressor; it must be demanded by the oppressed.

—Martin Luther King Jr.

You have to grow from the inside out. None can teach you, none can make you spiritual. There is no other teacher but your own soul.

—Swami Vivekananda

AUTHOR'S NOTE

The events are portrayed to the best of my memory, as amplified by research and my mother's recollections. While the account in this book is true, some names and identifying details have been changed to protect the identities of the people depicted.

Prologue

Dreamscapes and Nightmares

It was a recurring dream. A little girl standing in a crowded room with other little girls and four faceless women who wore long head coverings and long dresses. A house bursting with bodies wrapped in monochromatic fabric. A mother who wouldn't open her mouth for fear of retribution.

I dreamed these scenes, vividly specific, every night for ten years until I was fourteen years old, but I had no reference for them—no photos, no stories, nothing that I would have called a memory. Sitting cross-legged on my bed one evening, I wrote about that girl from my dreams. I felt I knew her, so at age fourteen, I went to my mother's room for answers.

"When I was small, was I ever in a room with dozens of other girls?" I asked.

My mother raised her eyes and took a pull on her Newport. I continued.

"Was I ever thrown outside? Did I speak fluent Arabic at one time, and you and I couldn't speak to each other because you only spoke English?" I asked. "Basically, was I ever hijacked?"

My mother breathed deeply and sat up straight.

"How do you know this?" she asked me. "You were too young to remember."

"So it's true?" I responded. "There was a beautiful, tall man named Imam Isa, who had long, bony fingers and intense eyes?"

My mother lit another cigarette and told me to sit down. She was crying.

PART ONE

Upside Down

One

Tell the Story

Old habits are said to die hard, and the same is apparently true for traumas. Beginning in earnest in 2016, the nation has been in a renewed fight against old themes and updated gaslighting techniques, reopening former wounds that had previously been sloppily sutured over. There was the target on Muslims preventing them from entering the country in 2017; the nation's formal child-separation policy in 2018, which removed children from parents; and in 2020, the explosion of the Black Lives Matter movement because of the constant police killings of Black people. I watched wearily as we moved from one crisis to another. Decades before all of this, I was acutely aware of what it meant to fight for freedom and belonging, and to lose a family at the same time. These traumas are irritatingly unhealed because they are cyclical, because this is not the first time that race has intersected with the systemic breakdown of families and the abuse of children.

Back in May 2002, when I was a freelance journalist in my midtwenties, I was following the story of a man named Dwight York, whom my parents and I once knew as Imam Isa. Other aliases include Malachi Z. York, Issa Al Haadi Al Mahdi, and Dr. York. I first came across a rushed CNN article reporting that York had been arrested in

Georgia on some heinous charges. At home, searching online at my tiny work desk, I eventually located a video of him standing in an orange jumpsuit with a white long-sleeve thermal covering his arms. He hung his head to the charges read against him: forty counts of aggravated child molestation with a maximum of thirty years in confinement for each count; thirty-four counts of child molestation with twenty years maximum for each count; one count of sexual exploitation of children with a maximum of twenty years; two counts of influencing witnesses with a maximum of ten years for each count; and a minimum overall of ten years of probation.

The hair on York's head was dark and knotty. The hair on his face was almost white. His attorney looked embarrassed, and the judge, peering over his wire-rimmed glasses, seemed vindicated. When asked by the judge if he understood all his rights—the charges brought against him and if he did what the district attorney accused him of doing—York nodded yes. When asked if anyone promised him anything, frightened or forced him into pleading guilty, he shook his head no. His mouth looked withdrawn inside itself. The judge asked York if he could hear and understand his questions and statements, and the old man nodded. Watching the video, I thought if I saw him in the world, he'd be mumbling to himself as he shuffled down a frigid New York City street.

A few days after I watched the video, I discussed it with *The Source* magazine's editor, whom I knew had taken classes with York in the past. He, too, knew that I had my own personal experience with York and asked me to cover the arrest. I thought it would be easy and forced myself to detach. Not only did I have historical knowledge of York but I knew he had hundreds of devoted followers. Some saw him as legendary. Before becoming Imam Isa, he was rumored to have been a calypso singer with a voice that hypnotized. In the 1970s, he founded the Ansaaru Allah mosque on Bushwick Avenue and grew it into one of the biggest mosques in the city. After becoming Imam Isa, people would say he had magical powers, levitated, could read minds. He was seen as otherworldly.

As a native New Yorker working as a hip-hop journalist, I had randomly met plenty of young Black men who had experimented with York's teachings at some point in their lives. Some attended his classes. Others simply read his books. Many knew someone who followed his teachings. Regardless of the vehicle, they were fascinated by the message and the execution. York was seen as a defiant man who taught Black people that they were descendants of Sudan who could govern themselves and one day would return to the nation, our rightful home, to do so. York's downfall interested the hip-hop magazine because he touted famous rappers as fans and followers.

Researching York's movements, I learned that he went from teaching his brand of Islam in Bushwick to moving his congregation to the Catskills in upstate New York in 1993 before heading to Georgia that same year as a cowboy, then as the Chief Black Thunderbird Eagle of the United Nuwaubian Nation of Moors, and ultimately as an Egyptian god and interplanetary citizen. I pondered the fact that more than twenty years after my mother and I left Ansaaru, York still had enough supporters to fill a small town. His teachings seemed to change as much as his name and location, but antiwhite hate and Black nationalism were the threads he needled wherever he went.

Several months prior to the swarm of federal officials that descended on York's Georgia compound in 2002, one of my mother's neighbors left her husband and children in Brooklyn to join his Nuwaubian Nation, which to me was akin to running away to become a big-top animal trainer. Like the dozens of other people who were said to reside there, my mom's neighbor lived in a trailer on 476 acres of packed dirt—surrounded by ankhs, obelisks, sphinxes, and other Egyptian motifs—that the residents called Tama-Re and that, after York's arrest, the media dubbed "Egypt of the West." In articles, some people said the then fifty-six-year-old York claimed complete control over the lives of his congregation. He rationed their food. Women weren't allowed to leave the compound. Sometimes there was no electricity. Soon there was talk that five children, as young as four years old, said he'd molested them, which was what finally led someone in York's inner circle to call the law.

The purported five children ended up being hundreds, and on May 8, 2002, about two hundred FBI agents and eighty sheriff's deputies dropped onto Tama-Re. Twenty weapons and $280,000 in cash were uncovered. Agents also reportedly found ten guns and $127,000 in cash in York's two homes in Athens and Milledgeville, Georgia.

Maybe a week after the compound was raided, my mom's neighbor returned home to her family. Still on assignment for *The Source*, I nervously went to interview the neighbor for my story, whom I hadn't seen since I started college nearly six years prior. She was polite but prickly when I lived at home. When I went to interview her, I stood in the hallway outside her apartment expecting her to welcome me in, but she peered out the cracked door and said, "I don't want to talk to the press about this, and I don't want to talk to you." Then she slammed the door and locked it. I remember staring back at the barrier, confused.

My mom said she wasn't surprised when I told her later how her neighbor reacted. "She's probably angry, embarrassed, or maybe she's so into it that no one else matters," she said. All of those explanations were really interesting to me.

That evening, I turned to my network and set to finding Nuwaubians in Georgia. Similar to my mom's neighbor, hardly anyone would go on record or speak on the phone about York. The people I found said they didn't want to be perceived as talking to the press, selling out, or dishing their filthy family business to outsiders and spectators. Very few trusted I'd honor their stories. Even fewer believed I understood the betrayal they felt, except for two very scared yet brave women.

The first woman wouldn't tell me her name, but she spoke fast and clear with a slight squeak. She was about seventeen years old. Her mother had followed York from Brooklyn, where they had been devotees since she was young. She said York had an appetite for girls, and mothers sent daughters to his house to procure food or whatever they needed that they didn't have. This girl said her mother handed her teenage sister over to York as a gift. She said she knew she was in a cult, knew that York just made things up to maintain control and feed his god complex. As was the case in Brooklyn, the teenager said the Nuwaubians had a daily quota of twenty-five to one hundred dollars to fill and faced expulsion if they came up short. She argued that York's shape-shifting philosophies were proof he was a charlatan, and she couldn't understand why the adults didn't see it. I remember telling her that adults can be selfish. And stupid, she interjected. She explained how they were supposed to be Muslims when stationed in New York but Native Americans who were waiting for UFOs to rescue them by the time she and her mother had moved to Georgia. Dressing the part didn't make it so, she explained.

The other woman I spoke with wasn't as forthcoming. She communicated with me through different accounts for a month, hesitating to share her phone number whenever I asked for it. When she finally acquiesced, the phone rang seven times before the woman answered, speaking in a hurried murmur and then hanging up. "I gotta go, my husband is home," she said. When he was out, she would email me again to call her. She breathed fear through the phone when she answered my call.

"We're forbidden to speak with the press or with anyone outside, so I have to whisper," she said. "If I hang up, it's because he's home. Okay?"

To relax her, I told her I knew all about York from his Brooklyn mosque. She, too, knew about Ansaaru Allah and maybe thought if I knew about his other religious iterations, I wasn't reporting to be scandalous. Then she talked.

"My husband is a believer, but I'm not," she said. "It's a cult. I believe York molested all those children like they say he did. I'd hear stories about him taking them when they started their periods.

Mothers giving daughters as gifts for special privileges. Just like he did in Brooklyn, he rationed everything here. There are about a hundred of us on this compound, and it's like we're living in the 1800s. There's no heat. Sometimes no electricity. We never leave the compound, and guards are always at the gates. I want to leave. The only reason we're still here is because my husband is a stone-cold supporter, and he's not alone. Many here are still trying to maintain York's teachings, hold down the compound, even though he's in prison. You can't tell these people he's wrong. His followers will hurt you if you do."

"What will you do?" I asked her.

"There's nothing I can do but pray my husband doesn't learn I'm not a believer," she said. "If my husband knew I was talking to you, he'd kill me. But someone has to tell the story. I can never tell more than I'm telling now."

I thought a lot about what that woman said—someone had to tell the story—and filed it away. I learned that even after York's arrest, many of his followers dug their heels deeper into the compound's foundation and the idea that an unlawful conspiracy had taken place against him and them. Months progressed, and as I continued to personally follow York's case, I would do no more than jot down thoughts on a notepad. After York initially argued that he could not be held in court because of his Native American heritage, he eventually pleaded guilty to child molestation charges in January 2003 and the following year was ultimately sentenced to 135 years for molesting countless boys and girls under the age of sixteen.

~

Four years after York's conviction in 2008, on a bright New York October morning, I was riding the train to work and reading a list of ten blurbs in *Time* magazine. Number five was about the FBI raid on Arkansas evangelist Tony Alamo, who was arrested for taking minors across state lines. Standing over my left shoulder and leaning against the train door was an older Black man in a Rasta-like hat wearing dark glasses on a bearded face. Hanging over his quasi-Israelite, quasi-militant garb was a neck-full of chains and medallions. Out of the myriad of clips on the page, he pointed to exactly where I was focused with one large, dirty fingernail.

"You believe that's true?" he asked me.

I nodded yes without looking up. I wish I hadn't.

"This is exactly how the government keeps us separated," he erupted. "You can't be a lamb in this wilderness, sista! They do this all the time, trying to break up the flock 'cause somebody's trying to teach us the truth! They did it with Waco, they did it with Jim Jones, and they did it with York . . ."

I ran off the train, nauseous. *Did he just say York?*

I took flight for the subway stairs with the man yelling at my back, "Don't be so naive by letting the government control you! Read about York, read about him!"

When I got to work, my dress was stuck to my skin and tears were welling. I called my mother; she always had the answers.

"You know I don't believe in coincidences," she said. "How is it that out of all the hours, minutes, seconds, out of all the trains in this city and all the cars and all the people, this man found you to say this to?"

"I don't know." I was annoyed and fascinated by the question.

"We're not the only ones who know things, Jamiyla. The saying that 'everything happens for a reason' isn't just a saying."

My mother's words ricocheted alongside those of the raging man from the train. Things happen for a reason. As a journalist, I needed to understand the innate, universal emotion of desperately wanting to belong and to feel free. As an individual, who was once a child forgotten by her own self until the memories of that ghost resurfaced, I had to know how York was able to amass power from so many parents, including mine. Were my parents honestly looking for Islam and naively fell into York's sweet-sounding narrative that, through separatism and the religion he taught, Black self-empowerment was ours? Did they take the devotion bestowed on York by other Black people at face value, without researching the group's background? Or was it enough to be a member of an exclusive group who bucked the system and created their own customs?

In the mid-2000s, when I was in my early thirties, I decided to go even deeper than I had in my reporting for *The Source* and face the ghost of my early childhood to better understand those dreams and memories I'd first confronted years ago as a fourteen-year-old. Over the years, through college and across country borders, the information came to me zigzagged, time-warped, and with delayed revelations and holes. I was too immature in my twenties to ask for help with those gaps but thirsted for it after turning thirty and continuously tried to quench the thirst by turning to my mother, Ummi, over the next couple of years with questions and curiosities.

For about a year during that time, she patiently sat through multiple interview sessions, in person and over the telephone, as I excavated, queried, and tape-recorded our story. I shared with her the fear that was shared with me by the women in Georgia a decade before and that cult leaders were still operating in groups like the Buddhafield, who had recently fled from Los Angeles to Hawaii. By then, I no longer dreamed of the little girl from the Ansaaru Community, which people, and I, lovingly called the Community, but they remained unforgettable. I couldn't shake the little girl, the same way I couldn't shake the helplessness and fear shared by the people with whom I had spoken to for *The Source* article several years prior. I was also ready to move beyond the persistent anger I had toward my mother, which began inside the Community in 1978 and rose to a crescendo in 2001.

Even though Ummi never ceased to confirm or correct my memory, she remained reticent, often admitting that she would rather have left the putrid bones of my dreams buried in the past. She said she preferred to move on and never look back, but I couldn't move on yet. I needed Ummi to understand that the Community didn't happen to her alone; I had been there too.

After witnessing four years of a presidential administration that heightened racial tensions, created a policy to separate children from their parents, and banned Muslims from traveling to the country, all while amassing a cult following that led to hundreds of white men storming the US Capitol on January 6, 2021, under the guise of having been disenfranchised, I saw too many parallels to the world of York. York was in prison for life, but the kind of desperation he fed on for decades remained. Many who agreed with Donald Trump's staunch stance against immigration argued that parents deserved to lose their children because that was the policy. I didn't think it was that simple, as I finally understood what made my parents separate from me and from each other in the late 1970s. Today, four decades after leaving the Community, I have since learned that the need to find the good in something is universal, even when what is found has devastatingly harmful effects.

Two

The Arrival

We were in the Christmas spirit when my mother did something she never did again. She decided to become a Muslim and then quit her job.

"I'm resigning, effective today," she told her supervisor James Perkins at Lane Bryant.

It was 1978. At the time, she missed the irony of being able to tell her boss James she was leaving but not her husband James, though the reasons she wanted to leave both were different. One hired her fresh out of high school and saw her work ethic as something he could cultivate; the other she fell for in high school and thought it was with him that she could build a life.

Her supervisor kept shaking his head. "You don't have to leave, Nancy. Your bookkeeping skills, your detail to inventory, your professionalism here these past two years have been an invaluable help."

"Thank you, Jim," my mother said. "I do like working here."

She started to tell this story as I sat cross-legged on her bed during one of our first interview sessions in 2006. The windows were open, and spring light was streaming through. I was squinting, struggling to create trust and exude journalistic professionalism, even though I was thirty and had experience interviewing all sorts of people. I was hoping

I looked at ease, despite the bead of sweat that ran down my spine. I had asked my mother to explain what she did after agreeing with my father to move into the Community. At first, she said, "What do you mean, 'What did I do?' I quit my job." She sat on the edge of her bed, toward the corner of a pillow, back straight, shoulders nipping at her ears. My question seemed to irritate her, like I was intentionally dredging up decisions that she now saw as erroneous and immature.

"Well, what did I do?" my mother said to me. I nodded.

She then recalled quitting her job. As she spoke, I envisioned her boss James scratching his head and looking closely at her twenty-one-year-old face, with her standing in front of him trying to portray confidence in a tan pantsuit. I see him ask her, "Then why are you leaving? Can you at least tell me where you're going?"

My mother huffed and said she didn't look him directly in the eyes. "I told him, 'I don't want to sound rude or ungrateful, but my reason for leaving is between my husband and me. As for where I'm going, I'm going to be a Muslim. That's all I wish to say.'"

"That's what you said?" I asked. I felt the urge to laugh at how dramatic her statement sounded but didn't. I was aware that I was asking her to get into the mind of a woman who was younger than I was at the time.

"Yes," she said without emotion. "That is what I said to him."

My mother honestly believed there was nothing more she could say in defense of the why. She thought the answer, *I'm following my husband*, was the absolute truth, even though it felt like a half lie to her. She wasn't going to admit her hesitation to her boss, that she didn't even know what it meant to become a Muslim, as she had said.

The open window let in a gust of air, and we both shivered. I wanted her to close it, just as I wanted her to shut the television off, but I was in no position to make additional demands. She was talking and I was going to listen. When I asked why she gave her boss that answer, she said she thought about the few friends she had and their repeated whys, she heard the husky voice of her gruff father calling her stupid for following a man he didn't like into an unknown world, and she couldn't stand to give anyone any more ammunition to judge her. She sat up straighter, pushed her shoulders farther back, and looked me directly in the eyes.

Seeing this defiance decades later, I imagined her boss James probably took a step back and sighed lightly, as though looking at something he once saw potential in but now couldn't reach. "Well, if you change your mind in six months, you'll still have a job waiting. I hope to see you back."

My mother said she smiled, shook his hand, and left. She walked away dry-eyed, stifling tears, having learned early on that instead of crying, it was best to stone her face and sheath her heart from unexpected blows. When she returned home to our Bronx apartment with its towering Christmas tree and stuffed animals strewn across its waxed wooden floors, my mother packed the only three outfits she had for her new life inside the Community into a small bag along with a box of sanitary napkins, a handful of panties and socks, and her toothbrush. Similar essentials were packed for me. My mother left behind the suits and shoes she'd accumulated for work—a place she could never shop at because the clothing wasn't cut for thin clients like her, which she liked because it kept her from spontaneous spending—and she stood in the middle of the living room meditating over the new life she was about to embark on with me, a two-year-old.

Having been told in advance by my father's God-sister Aaliyah that material possessions were not allowed in the Community, my mother left behind all of my toys and her handful of self-bought gold jewelry: a cross pendant on a necklace, pearl earrings, a peridot birthstone ring she believed had magical powers strong enough to ward off imminent nightmares of her living with a wicked grandmother who threw pots and pans at her head or beat her with wire hangers, and her beloved charm bracelet, cluttered with dangling hearts, bears, and two *N*s, one for her name and one for mine. Instead, she took what Aaliyah said was allowed: her silver wedding ring and the silver hoop for her nose, which had been pierced several days prior with a sterile needle during a quick trip to the Village. That day was the first day she wore the hoop and stared in a mirror, trying to visualize how different she would look in a few days when she could no longer press her long hair straight and wear it uncovered, flowing down her back.

Unwilling to part from baby photos of us, she stuffed hers and mine into an envelope to bring. There was also money, said to be of no use inside, but having it made her feel secure, even if she would never have a chance to spend it. She said she sifted out her Macy's credit card and her tax-return money, hid both in her bra. When she left the apartment with me trailing her, she walked away from her Christian name, Nancy, and the name—Nicole—she'd called me for the past two years. I, too, became a different person with a different name. Moving her long legs absentmindedly down the hallway, my mother neglected to tell the landlord his apartment was vacant and his lease broken. We never returned. I remember it being just the two of us. I assumed my father was already where we were going, probably shrouded in frankincense and myrrh and smelling of Egyptian musk.

Looking out the window during our hour-plus train ride to Brooklyn, with Yankee Stadium's huge crater cradling tiered seats and diamond-shaped dirt mounds to the west, we rode by high-rise buildings beaten dark brown by wind and rain into smaller family-style homes, each with their own personalities. Walking the five blocks to the Community from the Kosciuszko Street J train station, my mother kept squeezing my hand. Her tall, lanky frame seemed to rise to an unreachable height that was beyond my grasp.

When we got to Bushwick Avenue, we saw a street brimming with cars, whizzing down the narrow spine of two lanes, swerving to avoid deep-dish potholes. We walked past seemingly apathetic mothers who burned sage and sandalwood or who sprinkled Florida waterdrops the size of tears onto the backs of their departing sons to ward off the billy clubs and cuffs of bad cops or the gunshots that aimlessly traveled through their atmosphere. These moms shimmied to merengue or two-stepped to Motown while plantains sizzled in a pan or collard greens boiled in a pot. Big sisters sat on sepia-colored stone steps weaving rows of braids into smaller versions of themselves.

This live-out-loud world was not the one we were entering.

Upon arriving at the big white house, my mother pressed the buzzer and smiled when Aaliyah opened the door.

"Aquila!" Aaliyah said. I saw her eyes smiling between the material covering her head and lower face. "You're right on time," she said, giving my mother and me two kisses on each of our cheeks.

Pulling us in and closing the door, Aaliyah told my mother to put her bags down and offered us a tour of the multistory house. She explained to me all the adult women were to be called Um preceded by their names. I thought it was the same concept as when I used "Aunt" in front of one of my many aunts' names. From that moment, I also called my mother Ummi in place of the traditional "Mommy" or "Mom," though I have no memory of calling her either. My father became Abbu. I don't remember if anything was said about how to address other adult men. Um Aaliyah showed us everything from the kitchen to the prayer room in the basement. The last door opened revealed my new home.

"And this is where Jamiyla will stay with the other girls her age," Um Aaliyah explained. Ummi bristled slightly, and Um Aaliyah asked what was wrong.

"I'm confused," Ummi said. "My daughter is staying here in this room? Without me? I thought we would all move into an apartment."

"There are no apartments, just quarters with rooms," Um Aaliyah told her. "There's a Men's Quarters; I'll show you the Sisters', which is right next door because we keep close to the children; and this, as you now know, is the Children's Quarters. Abdul and I don't share space. No mates do, other than Imam Isa and his wives. That's just how it is."

"So, I will not be with my daughter?" Ummi asked again.

"No. No child is taken care of by their own mother. Imam Isa believes that would lead to nepotism, which is something we don't want."

"James couldn't have known this, right? Why would he withhold this?" Ummi asked, as if talking to herself.

"You mean Azim, Aquila?" Um Aaliyah corrected. "I'm sure Azim knew. He's been coming down here for months. He and Abdul speak often. He probably knew it would make you uncomfortable."

Ummi opened her mouth, probably to ask more questions, but then promptly closed it. I looked up expectantly for her pushback, which didn't happen. This was my first lesson in the importance of staying quiet. Once I was settled in my new space, without toys or a mother, with eight new eyes staring at me, Ummi told me to be good and then she was gone. She later told me Um Aaliyah led her back to the kitchen and handed her several stapled-together pages of questions.

"Before you can officially move in you have to fill out this personal profile application and have your photo taken for your ID card," Um Aaliyah explained. "You must wear your ID always. Just call my name when you're done with the form, and I'll come get you."

Remembering the form, Ummi said she paused at intimate questions asking how much money they made on the outside, what professions they had before, and how many times she and her partner had sex. Alarms went off as she flipped page after page of the two hundred inquiries until she decided to move through them as if she were asked such things daily. Oddly, it wasn't relinquishing care of her daughter to strange women or answering dozens of demeaning questions that caused her heart to drop to her stomach. It was when she was shown her spot on the floor in the building next to mine that she thought to leave.

Standing in the doorway with nothing except her small bag of clothes with her three outfits, a few toiletries, and the clothes on her back, Ummi described clotheslines crisscrossing the room like a constellation, folded-up cots, and crates on the floor doubling as drawers or a platform for a mattress. She wondered how six women slept in such a tight space. Turning to Um Aaliyah with her defiance doubling up on itself, Ummi said to her, "You don't expect me to sleep here."

Putting a hand on her hip, Um Aaliyah replied, "Aquila honey, there's no place else to sleep."

In disbelief Ummi asked, "Where is my husband sleeping?"

"In the Men's Quarters with the other Brothers. Remember, Aquila, you have to have an open mind, or this won't work. We humans are highly adaptable, and we learn to get used to things, like sleeping in a packed room. Believe me when I say it took some getting used to for me too. It wasn't easy, but this ain't supposed to be easy."

Ignoring Um Aaliyah's philosophical explanation, Ummi was convinced her husband did not know she had to rest her head in a ten-by-eight-square-foot shoebox of a space.

"Well, do you know where my mattress is?" Ummi asked. "James, uh, Azim shipped it a few days ago."

"A mattress? No, I haven't seen any floating mattresses," Um Aaliyah responded, probably looking at Ummi with confusion.

"It must be here somewhere, right? I see a couple mattresses in this room, so some people have mattresses. Maybe Azim has it?" Ummi pondered.

"Maybe," Um Aaliyah said. "Maybe. Until you can find it, the Sisters and I will do our best to help you adjust. I know it's a lot to take in and you must be exhausted. A nap may do you good."

"Thanks for understanding, Aaliyah, because it is a lot. And I am exhausted."

Ummi turned around the room slowly and placed her belongings in one of the corners as far away from the center as possible. Um Aaliyah called the women in who weren't working in the Children's House to meet Ummi, and they all greeted her as clones of each other, offering balanced kisses on each cheek and a welcome that sounded like *a'salamalaikum*. She was without a mattress, so some of the Sisters gave her additional blankets to ease the pain of the hard wood, and this made Ummi feel weirdly connected to the strange women. With the little means of comfort they could spare, the Sisters did their best to alleviate her discomfort, and she loved them for it. Yet after two days of sharing the already-crowded floor with mice and roaches, Ummi could not be sustained by the thin blankets provided by the sisters.

Three

Inside the Community

With eyes wide open, I walked into a room where four Ums stood covered from head to toe in yards of fabric. Even though they were hidden underneath hijabs and behind pulled-up *khimars* that were pinned behind ears, I could see their beauty reaching out through eyelashes that shaded serpent-shaped eyes the colors of caramel apples, raisins, walnuts, and steel. I could see the outline of their toes as their white tube socks swaddled their feet and heard the clanging sounds one of them made every time she moved an arm that was wrist-covered in fist-bumping silver bracelets fashionable at that time.

Instead of opening their hidden mouths to say hello, they simultaneously nodded their heads in silent acknowledgment. Even if I could have seen their mouths, I doubt they would've let the corners of their lips spread up into a smile, into the shape of kindness. Without reason or evidence, I didn't think any of these Ums had children. At least not here. They radiated disdain more than deference. If they had children in the Community who were being taken care of by women they didn't know, I thought these Ums would have been warmer and more maternal than the annoyed cut-eyes they gave, which made it clear we were not in this together. I doubted they would ever like me.

As if a curtain magically lifted, I then noticed about thirty other girls around my age in the room. We were all mirrors of each other, dressed in the same attire, with the headpiece pulled the same number of inches just above the similarly smoothed eyebrows that sat just above matching meek eyes. They were huddled in front of a small television that was playing a *Tom and Jerry* cartoon. Upon my entrance, their toddler heads craned in my direction with wonderment and curiosity. These girls didn't smile either.

Just as quickly as I crossed the threshold into my new life, Ummi was back in the room, collapsing her tall frame to my size and helping me out of my heavy brown shoes. Spotting the television and all the girls, she said, "Look, your favorite cartoon is on. And you have a bunch of new friends to watch it with. Not bad, huh?"

I nodded. I wasn't sure why it sounded like she was trying to sell this place to me, as though watching *Tom and Jerry* with a roomful of strangers superseded watching it at home with a stuffed animal stuffed inside the crook of my arm. I couldn't explain it, so I said nothing. I only nodded.

Taking this as a sign I was willing to soldier through this new adventure, Ummi laid a big kiss on me, wrapped her Isis wings around my stiff body, told me to be good, then turned around and left. Her legs lifted her out of the crowded room in two eyeblinks, making it so one moment she was there and the next she wasn't. Ummi didn't tell me who these people were, how long I had to stay with them, or where she was going that I wasn't allowed to go. She simply left me standing there, staring into the empty space she'd claimed several seconds ago, not knowing what to do with my voice or where to put my tears.

I didn't cry out for her because I was in a shipwrecked state, where up didn't matter from down. I thought she'd be back to tuck me in for sleep, as was our routine. I didn't know why, but I was afraid of these silent women. They felt different from the ancient aunts Ummi took me to for day visits, who practiced the words "french fry" with me until I got them right, even though I had more teeth in my head than they had in theirs. My young, their old, my matriarchs entertained me through sometimes mumbled, toothless stories of fights with ex-husbands and ungrateful children. I was at home among those older versions of myself who removed all masks and waved off sobriety once together. In the Community, however, there were no howling elder women who wore their hair in huge puffs or with sleek middle parts and who dangled cigarettes from their mouths while they swirled dark liquid in a glass of ice held haphazardly in a delicate hand. In this Community, there were no toys, no noise, no color.

Instead, when I looked around, I saw frost-white walls and a huge blue gymnasium mat covering most of the floor underneath a semisoft white light. My sadness lifted when I thought this was a playroom padded for hours of tumbling. The small woman with the stainless steel–colored eyes introduced herself and the other Ums—whose real names I have long since forgotten—and told me this was my room now. She suggested I take a nap. I stood still, twiddling the fabric of my dress, bunching it into small fists to let it out and do it all over again. I didn't want to nap. I felt my lips tremble and my eyes fill up. I said I wanted my mother. Words like lasers shot at me the instant I closed my mouth. Fingers clenched my chin and pressed into my jaw.

"Stop that nonsense this minute. We're your Ums now," the tallest one said, fingers squeezing. "Look around," she said, sweeping her sharp machete arm around the room, slicing through the stillness in the air. "Do you see anyone else asking for her mother or crying? No. You. Do. Not. And we won't have you being the one to do it either. Understand me?"

I didn't respond or lift my eyes to meet hers. I turned my attention back to the material and resumed making balls of crunchy fabric. The gray-eyed Um took my hand and walked me across the mat toward the silent audience. She patted me on the back and motioned for me to sit. Two girls made space enough for me to turn my bony knees into a pretzel under my dress like everyone else.

Soon, I too was quietly giggling as Tom chased Jerry away from a wedge of swiss cheese through the house before losing him, once again, to the mousehole Tom was too big to enter. I looked around for my own mousehole, but there wasn't one. The room didn't have many doors: a bathroom, a closet, and one to the hallway. I don't remember any other pieces of furniture except for the blue mat and stools or chairs the Ums sat on.

That night, a sticky feel and plasticky smell were what I slept on, in a labyrinth of feet to faces and knees to backs, all of us girls huddled together like newborn kittens. We had blankets but no pillows and instinctively used each other for comfort. Their body language confirmed there was no mousehole for any of us.

~

"Azim, where is my mattress?" Ummi asked my father when she saw him three days later. "I've been sleeping on the floor on a pile of blankets the Sisters gave me, and I can't do it anymore. Where's my mattress? Do you have it?"

My father replied in the negative and told her he also slept on the floor in a room crowded with mice and men.

"Well, it's somewhere. We sent it. And I want it back," Ummi said.

For Ummi, it wasn't so much about the loss of her mattress as it was about her feeling undignified. A rodent bigger than it should have been jumped out of a cabinet at her one day when she opened a door in the kitchen, and sleeping on the floor felt like being robbed. No daughter, no husband, and now no mattress. In all fairness to my father, she knew she was in over her head but was too proud to back out so soon. Plus, the thought of losing her family, of my father not standing with her, terrified her. Her upbringing had imprinted her with an unwavering belief that family was everything and anti-Blackness was everywhere, which meant that family had to stay together no matter what happened. These are the puzzle pieces that got my mother to agree to the Community, the belief that she would be able to make something whole.

Burning with youthful fire, America was at its wits' end when the 1970s rolled in, as was my father, who was beside himself about the injustices he'd seen on his television set while growing up. Missing out on the Black Panther Party's movement because they were an endangered species by the time he came of age, my father, an unwavering believer in Malcolm X and Marcus Garvey's Back to Africa movement, found what he thought was the next best thing to each of their teachings. Did my father not see that the separatist, divided-family policy preached by York wasn't what Malcolm, or many other practicing Muslims, had believed? Or did it not matter that York's Ansaaru philosophy was a dog-eared page torn from the idea of Islam because it filled a historical void?

I imagine my father was most drawn to participating in a separatist Black society because it promoted and promised Black self-sufficiency and Black man as king, neither of which were new concepts. Surely my father had been aware of Garvey's Pan-African Black Star Line, created to transport Black Americans to Liberia, where they would create a new settlement. Elijah Muhammad, who taught his Nation that the white man was the devil and one way to freedom was through economic independence, had been preaching this gospel since the 1930s, more than twenty years before my parents were born. In 1966, the year Stokely Carmichael declared "Black power"—disillusioned by nonviolent practices and integration as ways to end racism, instead saying that Black folks should take up arms—I know my father, who was about eleven years old, paid attention. By the time he learned about York in the mid-1970s, he probably saw Ansaaru as an extension of the movements that had come before.

The two decades after my father and mother were born, 1955 and 1957, respectively, were powerful ones. I can see myself in each of them. I imagine my eight-year-old father sitting in front of a black-and-white television set with his sisters, while my six-year-old mother nestled with others in front of hers the day after her sixth birthday, as Martin Luther King Jr. remade history with his "I Have a Dream" speech on the steps of the Lincoln Memorial. Three months later that November, that dream churned out a nightmare when President Kennedy was assassinated. Less than a week after my parents saw a grainy photo in the paper of the new president-by-default Lyndon Johnson signing the belated Civil Rights Act in 1964, as the good reverend stood over Johnson's left shoulder wearing a demure, knowing smile, the wild winds of racism didn't stop blowing, shortening fuses, and dropping young James, Nancy, and the nation into darkness because the scratchy signature appeased few. By the time three young civil rights activists were unearthed in Mississippi the following August—Mississippi's own James Earl Chaney and Andrew Goodman and Michael Schwerner from New York—I'm sure my parents mourned with the nation but more often than they would have liked.

The Vietnam War raged, a president who had championed Black folks' right to their inalienable rights was assassinated, and South Africa's version of America's King had been sentenced to life in prison for resisting apartheid. Black lives mattered little then, and the people wanted their power. When they moved to take it, it was sometimes close to home. So close I bet my nine-year-old father and seven-year-old mother were able to hear bricks crashing through storefronts, nightsticks falling bluntly, and the pop tunes of whizzing bullets during the 1964 Harlem uprising.

I wondered how they felt at those ages after learning of the fatal shooting of the Black fifteen-year-old James Powell by a white cop. I had read that the streets simmered for two nights with rage so incessant it flowed with the traffic all the way down the Hudson River and across the bridge to Brooklyn's Bedford-Stuyvesant neighborhood. Were my parents young enough to escape what must have been an inescapable heat? Harlem was the jump-off, the foretelling of the next several hot years to come, but what did they feel? How deep was the hole my father felt when his beloved Malcolm X was gunned down at the Audubon Ballroom on a cold February shoulder of a day, forsaken by men who looked like him? Surely he was forever changed.

When Watts flipped the switch again in August 1965, breathing a spark of life into the first Black Panthers, two Oakland college students, my father absorbed their ideology, as if by osmosis. Fury rippled across the country like a flag waving at high mast on a breezy day, and the young, Afro-growing James inhaled its rancor and stored it for some unseen future use. The devastating takedown of the King in 1968 insulated no city or citizen from the contagion called change, including my parents. Reeling from a feeling of helplessness and desperation, my father sought a revolution and focused on the Panthers as his kin, his skin. They were the faces he saw every morning when he washed his own, and he was determined to find their kind of liberty for himself.

Intrigued, my mother followed those radical college students with one eye squinted. Black power was my father's belief system; love was my mother's. Yet a decade later, in 1978, when my father came home and told her about this place called the Ansaaru Allah Community, that he had been taking Islamic classes in Bushwick and had finally decided to share his books about Muslims with her, Black power and love were the exact two motivations that turned them toward the Community's gates, albeit for different reasons. My father talked about changing his name, and my mother knew she had to hold on to that vision alongside him, for his eyes had become myopic, focused as one is when seeing blood on white tiles.

"We're gonna become Muslims," my father said. "That mosque I've been going to in Brooklyn, they've got it together. A plan. How we should live as Black people, and it's amazing."

My mother was happy he felt enlightened, but what she didn't say was she didn't want to leave her world for one she knew nothing about. She remembered my father stressing they wouldn't have to worry about work, shelter, or food to put in our stomachs. She was skeptical this was lazy talk. Growing up, my father was such a star that as the only male of five siblings, everyone in the family called him Papa, even though he was number two in the litter. My mother knew he wasn't the work-hard type.

Not telling her much more, my father did say, "I'm moving into this community with or without you and if it's without, it would be as if I didn't have a family." Blinking rapidly to hold in a feeling that felt worse than being asked for divorce papers, my mother thought that wasn't going to happen. She couldn't envision her husband leaving her and his small child behind for anything. She had the physical makeup of the family she'd prayed for, and she was not about to be abandoned again without some proactive action on her part.

My mother listened as my father, resolved, explained we would become members of a grand new family that would protect us from the evils of the white world. My mother liked the idea of joining a network of people who believed in the same freedom-fighting, do-for-yourself ideals she believed in. Whatever this place was my father described, it reminded her of how she felt about the Nation of Islam when she was growing up in Harlem. Powerful, private, and prestigious. She knew the only way she could become a Muslim woman and leave her world behind was with her family by her side.

To not be completely taken by surprise, she made several trips to the Community for classes, and my father took her to a woman in the Village who made Muslim clothing. She said she bought a white-and-green outfit for herself and the same for me. This was the extent of her interest. Everything else was done on autopilot. She pierced her nose at the place my father suggested, where he'd pierced his, feeling this was a brave footstep forward, and walked out with a string looped around her right nostril and the sterling silver hoop tucked away in a small plastic bag in her purse to be slid in later. She thought she was moving into a nuclear family structure where her husband and child would be close, and this was what she did not know until the day she arrived.

As a result of this emotional trespass, the mattress was just another unacceptable ping in her third eye and the one thing she felt strongest about. As a child living with her grandmother Granny, my mother shared a bed with Granny, balled in a knot at the foot in the corner by the window, while Granny slept at the head. She felt there was nothing my father could do about the rodents, but he very well could enlist his God-brother to help him drag a mattress into her room. While I was adjusting to sleeping with dozens of other girls, my mother was quickly learning to maneuver a twin-size cushion and a little cubby space for all her personal belongings. When I asked years later what it was like living there for two years as a married couple, as a woman, Ummi said there was no such thing as privacy.

"Let me start by saying I loved being around all those wonderful Sisters. What I didn't like was sharing a room with half a dozen of them. When you washed your undies, they dried out in the open on a line the Sisters strung up across the room. When you used the bathroom, there was no door lock. None of the rooms on any of the Community's floors locked except for Isa's, I heard, because the *mujahideen* policed the grounds twenty-four-seven. Everyone knew when you were on your cycle because our sanitary napkins were rationed, and if you needed more, you had to request it from the big house. Everything was controlled."

Ummi went on to explain the Community's philosophy. No one had anything to hide. What was good for one person was good for another, and if something had to be said, it was said to a roomful of people. Essentially, what affected one, affected all.

"The only time we weren't all out in the open was when we were using the bathroom or having conjugal visits. So you see, with all those restraints, I felt having a mattress was vital."

~

My dreams were rarely uneventful after I moved into the Community. I was back home with my family. My mother laid affection and sweet words on me before taking me to my aunts and grandmother who smoked cigarettes around slurred conversations that sometimes caused a mouth with golden teeth to fly out with laughter. Then I was at home with my mother, playing with toys and speaking to her because she liked when I spoke. I was home, back with my mother from the hospital, recently liberated from an arm cast resulting from an accidental dislocation from my clumsy uncle and the corrective iron leg braces I'd been Frankensteining through for months. I was running freely and happily.

When I awoke in the morning, and every morning thereafter, I realized my dreams were wistful imaginations, ghosts from a life I was barely remembering anymore but knew was real because it was. In the morning, the Ums and we girls made *wudhu*, the detailed cleansing of one's face and ears before prayer. Nothing about this process with thirty little girls was prayerlike. The Ums made three or four of us use the sink and tub at once while they stood over, inspecting everything we cleaned the way a butcher looks at meat he'd just cleaved to ensure he removed all the unnecessary fat. I learned taking one's time was as frowned upon as primping when an Um asked me to turn a wet palm up and smacked it with a ruler.

"The longer you stay in here taking more time than anyone else, the more licks you'll get," she said.

Once clumsily dressed in our identical gear, we lined up and headed to the prayer room in the basement to make *salat*, leaving our shoes behind. The basement, dark and stale smelling, appeared big with its wall-to-wall carpeting. A dim light hung from overhead, casting sinister shadows off the walls. The room was already stuffed with men, women, and children. I looked around for my mother or my father, but all I saw were replicas of one another, drapes of white, green, and brown fabric. Rough, curly, wildflower-growing beards. Various shades of brown skin combining into a painter's palette of inky tones.

I fell in place with the other girls in my group, behind the man known as Imam Isa—behind the men, behind the women, behind the boys. Last in line, I imitated the girls around me for how to pray, something that had me counting movements and tucking my toes so I could balance properly on my knees and not fall over as my head and cupped hands moved up, then down, from ceiling to floor. I strained to understand the words I heard, but all I got were sounds spoken from the base of Imam Isa's throat, with clicking inflections and long vowel stretches. I wondered who these people were and where my parents kneeled in this sea of churning chants.

Four

Settling In

There was no settling in. I didn't know if any of my mat mates felt more separated than unified, for how long they'd been there, or if they resented their families. They didn't ask me who my mother or father was or if I was afraid of our substitute mothers. I didn't know if they disliked oatmeal as much as I did, had brothers and sisters scattered throughout the buildings in different ages or gender units, or if they were alone like me. Like me, they might have been focused on surviving, unaware of when a new girl arrived because leaving was most important. To my quiet comrades, I very well could have been another pawn in a chess game none of us could ever checkmate.

As time went on, it became harder to remember a time without the same four Ums who became unflinching statues in my daily life. In the beginning, I rarely saw Ummi and saw my father even less. I believed he couldn't find me because I was always hidden in a stiff head covering. Hidden by my shapeless, starched, ankle-skimming dress. Hidden in the layers of a language I was quickly learning but barely understood at first beyond recitation. Not only did it feel as if the Community was trying to hide us from the world, it taught me that girls and women were not to be acknowledged except by other women or male family members. I didn't understand, even after being told that women and girls were too special to have everyone lay eyes on us.

I wanted to tell Ummi I would be happier, would smile more, if she let me sleep wherever she slept, even if it was on the floor. What I couldn't tell her was I didn't want to call the Ums anything resembling "Ummi." I couldn't tell her about my dreams of escape over the playground's circular barbed wire, where I would awaken in the same room, on the same flat blue gymnasium mat with someone's right foot in my face. One day, I remembered an Um said she needed me to stop looking so miserable. When I asked if I could see Ummi, she said no and whacked the top of my right foot with a ruler.

"You really need to get out of that," she said. "Do you hear anyone else asking for her Um? Anyone else looking sad all the time? You're not the only one missing somebody around here. Don't you think I miss my child?"

I didn't think any of our four Ums had children because if they did, why were they in the room with us all and not with them? Looking at this Um with her veil removed, I shook my head.

While I made some friends—girls I've forgotten the faces and names of except for pink, chubby-cheeked Latifah, who often wet the bed—and settled into the daily routine of making *wudhu* before *salat* in the prayer room, washing with two, three girls at a time in one tub, dozing with three dozen of them, it was brain shattering not seeing my mother.

When I asked years later what it was like for her, she said, "Time seemed to speed by. There was so much to take in and learn and get used to that weeks passed before I realized how long we had been there. I honestly didn't think we would stay as long as we did, but a day turned into a week, weeks turned into months, and the months became two years."

Unlike my days, where I learned Arabic at the mosque's school in the mornings, breathed afternoon fresh air in the playground, and watched cartoons at night before prayer and dozing, my mother's hours were consumed with learning foundational Islamic elements from a Sister who taught her that sounding like a proper Muslim was as important as learning how to make *salat* like one. No prayer was recited in English because the belief was that if Muhammad spoke to Allah in Arabic, then that was the language we spoke. The Ums and Abbus did everything they could to act, look, and sound like what they imagined Allah wanted of his disciples.

When Ummi was settled in weeks later, those who supervised put her in a small, windowless, cream-colored mailroom, where she responded to letters from inmates curious about Islam and the mosque. Word had spread from our gates to the gates of penitentiaries, and the Ansaaru Allah Community was gaining notoriety in its own Harriet Tubman, underground soldier way. With white paper and black ink, Ummi said she tried to answer their questions but felt like a fraud. We had been there a few months at this point, she had prayed more than she ever had, yet she was sleeping on a mattress on the floor. A guard was always close by, and there was one man who knew everybody's everything. What more was she going to tell anyone about the freedom of Islam? She knew that she knew nothing about freedom or Islam.

From pencil-written letters scribed with uncertain hands, Ummi could tell the inmates were starved for something. Insight. Direction. Proof of their potential. Just like Malcolm Little had, they were waiting for a savior and thought that savior was Islam or Imam Isa. If it saved Malcolm X from his drug, pimp, and theft game and gave him the self-determination to articulately debate any white man anywhere, then it seemed inherent Islam was their rightful religion as well. She knew that was what my father believed and didn't doubt herself that Islam could redeem and reform.

Ummi, however, was less confident whether Imam Isa's philosophy was true Islam. That was her intuition, but how would she know that the submission Islam required to Allah did not extend to Imam Isa and all men? She couldn't read Arabic, which meant she couldn't read the Qur'ans that were in-house. What mostly everyone read, alongside the Qur'an if they read Arabic, were Isa's books, which infused elements of Arabic into its English texts. She was also too embarrassed to ask anyone to read the Qur'an for her. When Ummi thought about other Black Muslims she was familiar with, like the Nation of Islam, whom she admired, she imagined that the Community—where she dressed like a traditional Muslim woman, heard Arabic everywhere, and adhered to an austere practice—was more authentic. Sitting in the windowless mailroom with its white walls, while she tried to respond to the letters, Ummi pondered all of this and the little she knew about Islam, even after being there for several months.

What she did know about the Community was that all adults worked but only a few were free to leave without questions. If they weren't doctors, lawyers, or nurses, anything that required them to go into the world, the women concentrated on childcare, cleaning, cooking, or working in the mailroom. Otherwise, it was to see a doctor, cash a welfare check, make welfare appointments. To get back inside, everyone had to show identification and a pass. Ummi's two-sided identification card showed two black-and-white versions of her. One side presented her dressed all in black with her veil down and the other with her veil up, which is what she would show the guards who weren't supposed to see the face of a woman to whom they weren't married. Unless a woman had a powerful connection in the Community, most sat like sardines in a can waiting to be plucked out by someone for something. The men, on the other hand, spent most of their days outside peddling. On the trains and in the streets, my father and his Brothers sold books and Imam Isa's words to the Black and brown.

Ummi used to wonder how Isa fed and clothed everyone until my father told her of a quota the men had to make every day before returning. She didn't know how much and didn't ask but learned if the quota wasn't met to the *mujahids'* satisfaction, they would expel the delinquent. Although Ummi never witnessed this, she'd heard entire families had been kicked out when the men were unable to make their numbers. She didn't hear anyone speak out against this because everyone knew if the rules weren't followed, they'd be excommunicated.

Not long after we arrived, Ummi started working in the mailroom. Before the Community, she worked at Lane Bryant. Trying to write the letters, Ummi thought of how she always worked and couldn't imagine my father standing in the street behind a cheap fold-up table selling for another man when he seemed unwilling to hustle a job for his family. Then she discovered he didn't always peddle. On a call with her maternal figure Mrs. Hargis one day, Ummi heard her say, "Sometimes James comes here for money so he can return and act as if he had sold books and incense all day." Angry, Ummi couldn't stand how he got to visit her adopted mother, probably take hot showers, and eat real food while she was trapped behind guards and gates.

Once Ummi realized my father would never be expelled if his Godbrother was a *mujahid* and he made his numbers, she learned survival wasn't about what one knew but who they knew. The skillful received extra provisions from Imam Isa or the *mujahids*, and if a woman was lucky, she could eat a queen's meal if Imam Isa summoned her to dine with him. There was also the rumor if an Um had a pretty daughter close enough to womanhood, she could use her as collateral, an offering to the prophet.

For those less savvy or too young to warrant interest, breakfast was Farina, Wheatena, or oatmeal every day. Meat for the women was rare, so they tried to stay full off fish, vegetables, and starch, sometimes without success. Worse off were the women who didn't have mates to bring them body lotion or sanitary napkins, which made them dependent on the Community for everything. Even worse was a woman whose mate didn't care if she had supplies or not. Where we children always had enough to eat, sturdy rubber soles to play in, and almost-new socks to wear, the Ums scraped for food or went without new shoes and clothes sometimes.

During a talk years later in her apartment, Ummi said that regardless of how impoverished everyone was, theft was common among the Sisters. She recalled that with few places to hide things, leaving belongings in the open was a risk everyone took. Ummi took a chance one day and hung her intimates on the clothesline because they couldn't dry in her cubby. When she returned, they were gone. The income tax money she had stuffed in her bra before we entered met the same fate. When she told my father about it, she was taken aback by how adamant he was on possessing it. He flexed his husbandly pecs, said he wasn't going to have his woman controlling the family's finances anymore; it just wasn't an Islamic thing to do. He told her he had proof straight from Imam Isa's teachings and the Holy Qur'an saying what was hers was his and what was his was still his.

Ummi thought about when she moved in with my father, who made more money than her but who went half on everything. She was so eager to show independence, she would struggle instead of asking for help carrying grocery bags home. There was so much to prove and to do: she was finishing her final year of high school, and though no one thought she would graduate on time, she did, while working and living as a wife. Paying half the rent, however, didn't safeguard her one day after work from finding an apartment her keys wouldn't open. Ummi didn't know what to do, so she stood in front of the door and waited for my father. Right then, she promised herself wherever she lived, the lease would be in her name.

As far as Ummi was concerned, when it came to the Community, my father had gotten everything when she agreed to move in. Yet she swayed on the tax return and gave him a fifth of it when she cashed the check during a quick doctor's visit. She didn't know why she wanted to keep it, as there was nowhere to spend it. That night when she went to sleep with the money under her pillow, she awoke the next morning to nothing.

"If I had that money, it wouldn't have gotten stolen," my father said. "I would've used it on something worthwhile."

"Like what?" she asked. "What do you need to buy, Azim?"

"A gun. I would have bought a gun."

"A gun! What in Allah's name do you need a gun for?"

"To protect us. We must be ready for a war, Aquila, at any given moment. You know the white man doesn't want us to have anything, especially freedom or the right to bear arms."

Ummi felt sad. We'd entered the Community to safeguard against harm, but inside they were buying weapons. It seemed too violent for a simple group of people who wanted to be good Muslims. My father told me once that all the Brothers had guns because a lot of people wanted to harm them. While probably true, the idea of a gun-toting Muslim seemed counterintuitive to the very idea of being a Muslim. The way people said "Hello," we said, "May peace be upon you." Carrying a piece wasn't synonymous with seeking peace. The rumors that Imam Isa acquired his real estate by terrorizing the original homeowners or incinerating the homes if people refused to leave or sell kept spreading. This rumor fueled their belief that we were being targeted.

We were as different from our neighbors as a lion from a lemur, but who were these people who claimed to love Black folks yet orchestrated terror tactics against them? Black love, white disdain, and cultural maintenance were messages drilled in our heads as we were told the only enemy we ever had to watch out for was the blue-eyed, dog-walking devil. In Bushwick at that time, it was an African American and Latino neighborhood with people who humbly accepted and respected the hidden Black folks in the mosque. However, if the rumors of Imam Isa's larceny were true, then it made sense my father believed we were at war.

Ummi didn't. Between the stealing and the Community's appetite for firearms, her antennae were shifting and reaching, sniffing out how much she didn't belong there. However, giving up less than a year in wasn't an option. She wasn't ready to admit they might have made a mistake. Losing face and her religion was worse to her than losing money.

Though Ummi questioned a kaleidoscope of unclear occurrences, she couldn't crack the biggest code—the man who brought everyone together. She rarely saw Imam Isa, and when she did, his presence was like a breeze blowing through branches. He was known to spend hours in his house, working in his recording studio making music or teaching tapes. Hearing him sing one day, the way his voice oozed like saccharine, Ummi understood why people thought he had magical powers. A sorcerer said to be fickle and paranoid, he was rumored to choose a woman one day only to banish her back to the cold wooden floors of reality the next. Ummi watched as women, even those with mates, threw themselves at him.

To many of the Sisters and Brothers, Imam Isa was a prophet. If he never said that we could live, many of us would have died. Women wanted to be with him, and men wanted to be him. If he said we were supposed to fast for three months and three days, we would have starved until he told us to eat. Ummi swore Imam Isa's nose could sniff discontent when spirits sank. She said it was then, in addition to *salat*, when he would emerge from his fortress and mingle.

One day he started a water fight between the men and women. Another time, they had a flour fight. All of them, dressed in the few clothes they owned, threw white powder back and forth, laughing and screaming as though they had forgotten how fun fun was. They were children again, but their laughter was a strange sound in the house. Even to Ummi's own ears, her happiness sounded odd. Everyone had a good time that day, but after all the mess was made, the women were left to clean the fine dust off the walls and from between the wooden floorboards, handwash their garbs, and panic over what to eat that night since they wasted all the flour on child's play.

Five

Tifl Time

The air was porous with infection and want. I saw Ummi twice a day during *tifl* time—a four-Um-supervised forty-five-minute visit. My first one, the Ums made me scrub down until it hurt, dressed me in my cleanest, and filled my belly. When I knew ahead of time that I was seeing Ummi, I paced and practiced my Arabic. I looked out the window for a sign my mother would say, *Enough*.

As Ummi crossed the threshold from the hallway into our room, looking like she was floating across the wooden panels, I noticed how her towering figure seemed to tower for only a second. It was brief, but I noticed it. Upon seeing her, my Ums' eyes narrowed and their bodies stiffened. In return, Ummi scanned the room before resting cautious eyes on the women who stood with their backs against an opposite wall. There was something kinetic in the air. It lasted a second, but the moment felt frozen in time. Then with a few strides, Ummi's legs carried her to the women, to the Ums I felt exuded so much power and control that Ummi looked as if her straight back curved and her shoulders secretly stooped, tricking the eye to make her shrink several inches in their presence on purpose.

"A salaam alaikum," Ummi greeted them. She gave two-cheek kisses to them all.

"Walaikum a salaam," they replied in unison and returned the affection in kind.

Civility shown, Ummi walked to me and made herself my height. She looked me in the eyes and I stared back, trying to remember what her hair, her shoulders, and her arms looked like. She pulled me close and in a low, soft voice said loud enough just for me to hear, "I love you, and Abbu does too." She didn't want the Ums to know she was speaking English, and when they moved closer, she quickly returned to her choppy Arabic phrases. The few times I had seen my father, I noticed he developed the authentic inflection and phonetic flourishes of someone accustomed to articulating consonants from the back of their throat. Ummi, it seemed, put less effort into converting her tongue than she had to converting her appearance.

I took in her difference. The fingers that were always adorned with rings were bare except for the fourth of her left hand. It didn't dawn on me the Ums all wore a silver hoop in their right nostrils until I saw Ummi with hers. Before moving into the Community, Ummi wore gold. Inside, everyone wore sterling silver because Imam Isa said gold was associated with royalty and vanity, both of which were forbidden. She also smelled like my Ums, sweet and musky.

"How are you?" Ummi asked in Arabic.

"Fine," I said, hoping my bowed head betrayed the words. I remember thinking how swaddled I felt, how she once anticipated my hunger, my mood changes, my caution; but here, for some reason, she didn't see me. After running out of things to say, she sat on the floor with me cradled in the dip of her crossed legs, hugging me until our time was up.

Some days in the Community I awoke thinking I would never see Ummi again, have a lollipop, or chew bubble gum until my jaws hurt, which Imam Isa forbade, saying it contained pork. I wanted to watch cartoons in a living room with my parents sitting behind me on a sofa.

I wanted her to say she loved me loud enough for the Ums to hear. But Ummi didn't say *I love you* out loud, which made me think those words were meant only for me. Her eyes watered during this meeting, turned into a well of emotions that trapped something helpless. This sorrow, this drowning, became the way we communicated.

~

As a thirty-year-old adult, sitting in Ummi's kitchen, listening to her tell me these stories, I still felt like a child. I had lived on my own since I was nineteen, but I spent years feeling intimidated by her and one link away from being close to her. Figuring out the right thing to say that wouldn't sound disgruntled or begrudging was a challenge, because I was both at the time. I sensed my mother was holding back, flipping through cutthroat words like cards to decide which one to use, what to say so that it had the impression she wanted to create. On this day, the kitchen felt smaller. I felt smaller, afraid to ask about specific childhood moments of mine—hesitant in my own self-inquiry and wondering if I were asking things out of curiosity or personal confirmation that I had crappy parents. The overhead light emitted interrogation-room glare. The wooden chair was hard against my back and butt.

Ummi put down two cups of steaming lemon tea and said it was hard for her to remember, talk about, admit the Community happened. She remained standing, holding on to the top of a chair with both hands, the bejeweled rings on her fingers gleaming. I shifted in my seat, pulled a knee close to my chest. Ummi opened her mouth to speak but said nothing. The sun was setting a crimson orange across the Manhattan skyline and shot sunlit darts into the room that cut narrow shadow lines across her face. Still quiet, the flip-flop sound of her sandals filled the air as she walked to the window, closed the curtains halfway, turned to retrieve a jar of honey from the cabinet to put in her tea, and returned to her standing position behind the chair.

"Even though I struggled with my tongue tied, my mind racing for words I hadn't learned yet, I was not about to break the rules," Ummi began. "So, doing only what I knew to do, when I saw you, I would hold you as if I had nothing else to hold on to. You looked so sad I felt as if my heart had been punched out of my chest. You didn't smile, you didn't laugh, you were a completely different child from the one who entered those doors. And when I would ask the Sisters who took care of you about your change, they always said you were happy, talked a lot. I had to trust them."

I scoffed. It was all I could do to stop myself from telling her she had made a mistake to trust those women over her own maternal instincts, if that's a real phenomenon.

"I had been working in the mailroom for some time now, but it wasn't working for me," Ummi recalled when I asked what eventually started to bother her, the tape recorder recording. "I needed to be closer to you and knew you needed to see me. Before my eyes, you transformed into the little girl I used to be—quiet, watchful, hesitant."

"That was me," I said. I shifted in my chair.

"Then there were times I spied on you when you weren't looking, to see if they were telling the truth, and when you were with the girls, you seemed happy—laughing, playing, talking—like the child I remembered." I didn't believe her. Maybe she had forgotten what a genuinely happy child looked like from inside the Community, where I doubt that many of us would have said we were happy.

"I didn't want you to think I just disappeared, and because the mailroom was in a different building entirely from the Children's House, my mission was to get next door in your building. Understand?"

I nodded yes, unable to speak. I thought she was fine with the Community's system because we stayed for so long, but she wasn't fine with it; she was trying to cheat it.

"After learning your father didn't have to peddle as much as others, after watching him personally talk to Imam Isa after prayer like they shared stories, after watching him make magic through his God-brother, I told Aaliyah I wasn't the right person for the mailroom. Aaliyah worked in the Children's House with the infants, and I asked her for help. I said, 'Aaliyah, I know I've not been here longer than other Sisters, but I'm unskilled for the mailroom and I really need to be closer to Jamiyla.' I asked if she could do anything, knowing she could pull strings.

"She said, 'Let me see what I can do.' That night I was in the Children's House."

Ummi remembered her joy of being in there. She loved the babies best. She would say there was something pure and godlike about babies. She believed they saw and spoke to angels. I knew she loved being surrounded by the small, squirming newborns, though it still sent a pang of jealousy through me decades later that she took care of others not her own. Luckily for her, there were a lot of babies to keep her busy. One room had four cribs, and one crib housed at least two infants. These creatures were godlike to Ummi, but they were not exempt from the Community's cluster culture. Huggies, Luvs, and Pampers cost too much, so she dunked their diapers and washed them by hand.

"Whenever the babies had something wrong with them, we Ums in the Infants' Ward became their mothers, pediatricians, and their loudest, most faithful cheerleaders," she told me. "We made saline solution drops whenever they had eye, ear, or nose infections. We nursery Ums worked around the clock because lots of germs went around, and being so small and vulnerable, the babies seemed to stay sick more than not."

One day, Ummi noticed some of the babies had little bumps that looked like whitehead pimples. She knew it was impetigo somehow. The disease begins benign but grows until it bursts, weeping contagious juice into the air to form a honey-crusted coating on its victims. She saw this happening in the ward, an outbreak, and this was when Ummi, her colleagues, and the babies were quarantined for a month.

"All infected babies were put into the smallest room of the Children's House, suffering there until healed," Ummi said. "This room was only big enough for two cribs. I'd never seen so many sick babies before. The room was a rotation of crying, irritated, lonely little ones no one wanted to be near. I volunteered. Who could have loved them in their puffy-faced ugliness better? I understood isolation and abandonment from living with Granny when I played games with an imaginary friend and went to bed often at two in the afternoon, sometimes without anything to eat as punishment. I knew about isolation."

Ummi went on to explain how few friends she had growing up because of Granny, who didn't allow company. The strange way she dressed after Granny put her in public school but didn't buy her any clothes, so she would knit skirts for herself made from different colors of yarn to try to fit in. Every year in school she had a different group, searching for the clique that would click. Ummi was familiar with being an outcast.

"As for those babies, I felt it was my duty to nurse those sick, rejected beauties back to health," Ummi resumed. "Twenty-four hours a day, seven days a week, it was just the babies and me. A bathroom close by with hot water. No one was allowed in and I wasn't allowed out until the final infant was released, happy, gurgling, and impetigo-free. The fear I felt kept me awake. But then I thought about you. Sure, I was self-sacrificing, but what about you? I could have gotten sick and then infected you."

I used to wonder what Ummi did in the Community that was so important she couldn't be with me. Maybe I would have thought she was a goddess, a lifeguard for angels, had I known she was caring for the smallest of us all.

"I worried about you so much during the outbreak," she recalled. "How could I live with myself if I harmed mine because I was helping others? But it never happened. Even though I was quarantined in that room with those babies, the most bumps I ever had was one or two. It was like a testament to how much I loved them. They kept me going because I couldn't have you."

They were lucky to have had her. The Ums who cared for my crew never cooed or coddled us. If one of us didn't feel well, they didn't work around the clock to make us feel better. They didn't sweet-dream us to sleep.

"Because I was missing precious time, I would sneak into your room when you were dozing and rock you to sleep, often," Ummi said. "You may not remember, but I used to sit on the long spiral stairs in the Children's House rocking you. You have no knowledge of this because while you remember some things, you don't remember everything. My thinking was, if I couldn't have you, I at least wanted you to fall asleep in my arms. I at least wanted my heart to be the last one you felt beating when you drifted off. I wanted my image in your dreams, not fear."

I often dreamed of being in Ummi's arms, her kissing my face. These dreams, though, weren't anything I could hold on to or get emotional nourishment from. I believed Ummi was telling the truth, that she did everything she could to be near me, but that didn't matter then, as nothing mattered more than leaving. Hearing that she had to sneak in to rock me to sleep did not make me feel any less resentful about losing months of my life with her.

"You can't imagine the privilege I had of being able to cradle you to sleep," she said. "And it was met with a lot of envy and frustration from many of the other Sisters."

I thought to interject, *Privilege? Envy? You sound crazy!* But I didn't. I let her continue.

"They didn't like that I was there just to hold you. Those who didn't work in the Children's Quarters didn't have that luxury," Ummi said. "When time was up, time was up; no matter how much they begged or cried, screamed or fought, the Um had to leave and couldn't return until it was visiting time again. But I had the advantage of working in the Children's House, and I wasn't giving that up for anyone. I used my presence in that house to see you as often as I could, even if it meant sneaking."

My thoughts drifted as I wondered if that was the reason the Ums weren't nice to me. The reason why I always felt I saw some slight tension between them and Ummi. She said we had received special privileges, but I hadn't felt special. Ummi had said she was against breaking the rules, yet she was talking about sneaking, which meant she did break rules and could have crashed the system to take me if she wanted. I didn't ask her to clarify. I listened as she told me that because she couldn't speak to me, she spoke to the babies instead.

With them, she didn't have to worry about English or Arabic or asking a question and getting nothing back but the blank stares she sometimes got from me. She invented her own language and spoke nonsense to them while they babbled back in the same nonsensical way. As a mother, she knew working with the babies caused resentment, and she empathized. For her own sake, she was terrified of becoming pregnant in the Community and then having to hand her baby over the way these moms did. As soon as new mothers left the hospitals, their babies went straight to her. From newborn to six months, Ummi was the Um they knew. Their mothers were only allowed to nurse them. When these discarded mothers did come, they greeted Ummi with glacial glares. Many mothers fought for peace with their babies because they had become strangers, and they blamed Ummi. Some even accused her of mental kidnapping. I asked Ummi how that made her feel.

"I admit if I had been told I couldn't work in the Infants' Quarters anymore, I would have lost it," Ummi recalled. "I would have clawed and screamed, snarled and bit until that person understood the infants and I were inseparable. If I couldn't be near my own baby, I wasn't going to miss out on being around babies altogether."

I was too stunned to say anything, too emotional. She found solace in taking care of other people's babies instead of her own, even as those babies' mothers despised her for assuming the role with joy. I don't think Ummi knew that story would have made me feel even more abandoned than I had felt, and her naivete was confounding. For her, the sentiment was simple—she loved babies and got to take care of a bunch of them at once, which meant that she was also busy. There wasn't much time for her to reflect on her own parental gaps.

About a year into living in the Community, Ummi said she frequently found herself sitting outside on the back steps, looking up at the stars and talking to God. Her head lifted, wondering at the night, she felt strongly if she stopped speaking to the God she had come seeking, then moving in, converting, inoculating against impetigo infections, the silent whispers she gave me—all would have been for naught. She really needed to believe, and she hoped that she had made the right decision. As long as the family was close, together somehow, she felt she was doing the right thing.

Six

A Portrait of Parents (1960–1977)

My mother shared a story with me where she remembered being three or four years old and in a living room watching *The Wizard of Oz* with her mother. Then, she was staying with her half sister's mother, Jean. My mother was running down the stairs to go outside to play when she bumped into her mother, who was coming to pick her up. My mother's next memory was being told by her father that her mother wasn't coming back. She had gone to heaven. Then my mother is dressed all in white. Her daddy picked her up, told her to kiss her mommy and say goodbye because she wouldn't see her again. She kissed her mother on the nose. My mother believed her mother had spoiled her because she had her own room and all the toys and stuffed animals she wanted.

My mother remembered going home after her mother's funeral and looking out a dark window to see her mommy go up to heaven, but she doesn't remember crying. She was five and turned six that year. She didn't have a party and knew from that moment she was an outsider who would always want a family. She was living with her half sister's family and jealous of her cousin Samantha, who was her age, because Samantha's class always went on trips. Even still, my mother enjoyed spending the night at Samantha's house watching Saturday morning cartoons. At Jean's, she slept three in a bed yet she still felt lonely. No one talked about her mommy or asked my mother how she was doing. To my mother, it was like her mother never was. She honestly couldn't recall thinking about her mother then. Maybe my mother was in denial.

One day, a man from the block took my mother and a trunkful of her clothes to her grandmother Granny's place. One moment she was in Brooklyn on Sackman Street and the next she was on West 153rd Street in Harlem. She was seven years old and going into the second grade. There were no children at her grandmother's, which meant no distractions and that she could no longer deny her mommy's absence. With Granny, she joined the Catholic Church and went to a school run by priests and nuns. School amplified her loneliness; she was surrounded by other children who had mothers, fathers, sisters, and brothers. Granny didn't allow friends over, and my mother couldn't go to their houses. She loved going to school to be around other kids because at home, it was yelling, with Granny saying, "You never going to be anything, you are so stupid." Granny always said my mother's mommy was a drunk who drank herself to death. My mother was Daddy's Little Girl until suddenly, like her mother, he was gone.

Her grandmother never told her she was pretty, so she started from a young age trying to dress up the outside to make people like her. She stole her Aunt Ramona's charm bracelet and left it in her desk at school to wear every day. When it disappeared and Aunt Ramona found out, she made my mother get in and out of a tub of water as she beat her. It didn't stop my mother from stealing. Next, she took Aunt Ramona's diamond ring and was busted by Granny as she was running down the stairs to the after-school program. Granny saw the sparkle, the ring on my mother's finger, and gave her a beating.

My mother will never forget her fifth-grade teacher, Ms. Noel. They had a Christmas play every year, and Ms. Noel picked her to be in it. Not one of the prettiest or smartest girls, but my mother. She thought Ms. Noel saw a frightened child who came to school with knots on her head and a swollen jaw and took pity on her. One day, after noticing the left side of my mother's mouth was swollen because her back teeth were growing in—she had never been to the dentist—Ms. Noel paid for the dental visit. My mother didn't visit a dentist again until she was a teenager and paid for it herself.

Growing up, she hated her grandmother and felt justified. Granny would wake her at five in the morning to do laundry before school and oftentimes told my mother that she wasn't going to school because she had to help clean white people's houses, with Granny always giving her the bathrooms to clean and clothes to iron and mandating that she get on her hands and knees to scrub the floors. Sometimes the bathrooms smelled so horrible, my mother felt she would throw up. Regardless of where they cleaned, Granny would threaten my mother, "Don't you steal anything and make me lose this job. I'll kill you." If there were random pennies or dimes on the floor, Granny swore it was a trap for her. My mother didn't take money, but she would take cigarettes from a dentist's office they cleaned once a week. He had cartons of different kinds in his supply closet, and Wilson became my mother's brand when she was in the eighth grade. She smoked cigarettes to look cool around the cooler kids and to defy Granny. She didn't think anyone cared about her anyway.

Her mother had died, which to my mother meant her mother didn't love her enough to want to live. She was with Granny because she had nowhere else to go—her father preferred to chase women—and Granny always told her how little she mattered. "You're tall like your father and just like him," Granny would tell my mother. "You're not going to be anything, like your mother. By fifteen, you'll be pregnant or in jail." Terrified of Granny, my mother kept her keep by doing everything her grandmother didn't want to do. Granny never went to the number's runner or asked to borrow money herself, so my mother would at Granny's behest. She would soak Granny's wrinkled, twisted feet in a shallow metal pan and scrape away the dead skin. My mother chewed her own nails down to nubs but took care when cutting Granny's. The only time Granny complimented her was when she washed her hair or massaged Granny's veined legs. Then, Granny would tell her, "You have strong hands, Nancy."

My mother took care of Granny, and while my mother suffered through a lot of colds, she didn't go to the doctor. Once she had a bad itch on her back but, afraid to tell Granny, she relieved herself with hot baths. When she got her period, she protected herself with rags, not sanitary napkins, which was no protection at all. For my mother's eighth-grade graduation, Granny let her go to the hair salon and get Shirley Temple curls. Sitting in the plastic chair, as an older woman applied a hot comb to straighten her hair and then pin curl it, she wondered if her father's then girlfriend, Mrs. Hargis, had paid for it. Granny was always taking money from Mrs. Hargis, my mother thought, who generously gave whenever Granny said my mother needed something.

What my thirteen-year-old mother needed, Granny believed, was a psychologist, so she dragged her to one. "She is crazy and a thief," Granny had told the doctor. During this time, my mother's older half brother, who was then addicted to heroin, stole from everyone. He would crawl through windows, break door locks, swipe wallets and watches. One day, after my mother and Granny returned home, Granny told her to turn the TV on. But there was no TV. Granny accused my mother of stealing it. My mother wouldn't admit to her therapist that when Granny beat her, she did so with my mother naked, her hands and feet tied, but she would say she stole whatever Granny said she stole, fearing Granny would beat her if she ever told the truth. Stealing was my mother's salve but not from Granny, who had nothing that could satiate her. Traveling on trains, my mother didn't fear putting her hand in someone's pocket to take money. When Granny sent her to the store over the Harlem River, across the Macombs Dam Bridge to the Bronx, she walked looking down to see if she would find money or sweets.

Once, she picked up a piece of candy off the ground and ate it. She was always hungry, always searching.

There were times when she tried to mentally summon her father, her hunger for a parent was so great, but as brief as were his visits, his anger was as quick. Instead of spending his visiting time with my mother, my grandfather and Granny would argue. He would curse her out and slam the door as he left. Incensed, Granny would then tell my mother, "Your no-good father, that son of a bitch." She would yell how she nursed him back to health when he was a baby because his own mother died from tuberculosis. My mother used to wonder if Granny said those things to confuse her or if they were true. If they were indeed true, was that the reason Granny despised her?

From ages seven to fourteen, my mother lived with Granny until she moved to Savannah, Georgia, with her father and to an alternate universe. She straightened her hair, wore makeup, and got attention because of her New York roots. She could make and receive phone calls and go to friends' houses. She never invited them to hers because she was ashamed of where she lived. As at Granny's, she had no privacy in Savannah. A curtain separated the bedroom from the living room where she slept on a fold-up bed. Anything said anywhere in the small house was heard by everyone else. She wasn't living with her father for long before learning he was a different version of Granny. He would call her bitch, whore, and one time he threw a phone at her face. He hurled its hard beige base and handset at her head, but she caught it before it could make contact.

It was 1971 and she was fourteen. The school she and the neighborhood kids attended was far away, so they got bused to the suburbs, to the white folks' part of town. Many would have thought that the civil rights movement for desegregation had died, but it still had a pulse, beating under the roof of her school. Before classes let out, a race riot roiled down the halls, clashed against classmates, and beat down the door of the principal's office. Standing outside, the neighborhood kids waited for the bus to take them home, but it never showed. Not knowing what to do, my mother followed the others who took off for the woods, running as fast as they could through thick trees and loud leaves, busting out at a mall and stopping short. Her heart was beating hard now for different reasons. A line of state troopers had their guns raised, pointed directly at them. She didn't remember anything after that or how she got home. When she and the other Black kids returned to school days later, the white kids threw rocks at their bus. She remembered their faces and her fear.

Though neither her grandmother nor father had ever talked about the Black Panther Party, she was interested in them because they were Black, because they focused on caring for and protecting the community, and because they believed all people should have power. She liked Muhammad Ali—the way he spoke, his self-confidence—but Granny didn't; she said his mouth was too big and that he made Black people look arrogant, so they never watched his fights. My mother didn't know how to voice her opinions, but she loved to see her people do it. They spoke for her.

Through the racial tension in Savannah, she focused on doing what she did best. Every Saturday morning, she cleaned the kitchen, bathroom, living room, and the adults' room before going out. She went to Catholic church in the morning, sang in a Baptist choir in the evening, and performed with a secular dance troupe in between. When she got to Savannah High School, she started paying attention to sun-kissed boys who showed self-pride with perfectly picked Afros. She didn't know what pride looked like up close when she was sheltered at Granny's in Harlem, but once seen, she never forgot it.

My mother was in Savannah for eleven months when she came home to find her father gone. No goodbyes, no explanations. She packed his and her clothes and boarded a train back to New York City with money Mrs. Hargis wired to her. Her Uncle Sammy and Aunt Pat met her at Penn Station's Amtrak, toting her father's green suitcase, and took her to their home, where she stayed briefly. Like a rolling stone, my mother went from living with her aunt and uncle to living in Brooklyn with Mrs. Hargis to back with her uncle, then back to Brooklyn. Wherever she lived, she slept in the living room and learned to pack in ten minutes.

My mother met James Chisholm at Brandeis High School. She thought he was cute and dressed his butt off. After they met, he would visit her in the Bronx where she was staying. He introduced her to his cousins and aunt who lived in the same projects she lived in. My mother was smitten and they started going together, breaking up when she saw him with his other girlfriend. The summer she turned sixteen was the summer she first experienced drugs, trying to fit in with the cool kids. Around June, she didn't know what a roach was to smoke; she thought it was a roach that crawled on the floor. By August, she was drinking a quart of Olde English 800 every night, and reefer stopped affecting her.

That summer, my mother got her first job as a camp counselor while living with her father and Mrs. Hargis in Brooklyn, who later adopted her as her daughter. She had no friends in Brooklyn and would hang out uptown with random people. It was the summer of "Let's Get It On" and "Rock the Boat," and she and her friend Amber threw a house party for each other's birthdays in a basement they rented. My mother invited James, who she then called Chisholm. When she spotted him swagging up the street in his soft suede and leather, she yelled his name, went outside, and ran right up to him. They got back together that night. Though she lived in Brooklyn and was at his house in Harlem more than hers, he always rode the train home with her. She thought he was thoughtful.

To keep up with him, she got a job so she could buy clothes and shoes. She put a rabbit coat on layaway because Chisholm had one. It was Christmas, and she also wanted black over-the-knee boots but couldn't afford them. She asked her father for help and he said no, leaving her stunned. My mother knew he didn't work but took money from

Mrs. Hargis like a pimp. She bought her own clothes, shoes, bras, and underwear and even paid for her own dentist visits, so she wondered, What could her father tell her? She went to school, to work, then to the Chisholms', and felt the least her father could do was help her get a gift for herself.

It didn't matter. Her father left Mrs. Hargis to shack up with another woman, so my mother bounced around again. When she had nowhere to go one evening, Mrs. Hargis welcomed her back. Mrs. Hargis must have told my grandfather that she was there because he called, threatening to beat her Black ass. She walked out the door that night with the clothes on her back and went to her friend Yvette's home, where she wore her friend's too-short pants until she could afford to buy new ones. No one knew she was there. Yvette's mother, Ms. Blackmoor, understood and got a fold-up bed my mother and Yvette took turns sleeping on. Finally, my mother had a sister and a family. She didn't know it then, but she was prepping to share space in the Community's makeshift household.

Unlike the Community, Yvette's mother made her open a bank account but never took the money. Instead, my mother gave her twenty-five dollars every week when she got paid to put into her savings account. Ms. Blackmoor called my mother's grandmother to ask permission to adopt her, but Granny forbade it, as though the very idea of someone else wanting her was unimaginable. My mother worked in the Garment District and was so detailed and fast she got more responsibility, like locking up at night. She didn't know by law she was too young to work machinery. Life felt good enough for her to realize she didn't want to be what she was becoming. She was still seeing Chisholm because he made her feel loved, and his family welcomed her as one of their own. They planned to live together after my mother graduated.

Ms. Blackmoor had a younger husband whom neither my mother nor Yvette liked because they knew he stole money. Once, my mother caught the blame. No longer comfortable at Ms. Blackmoor's, who wanted her in at 9:00 p.m. on school nights and said the next time she came in late she better bag her clothes, my mother did just that with Chisholm at her side.

They moved in together, and it didn't take long for him to become nasty. He called her bitch, whore, told her he was going to kick her ass. Somehow, my mother had fallen in love with a man who sounded like her father. Their relationship had become as volatile as the relationship she'd had with her father. One night, when one of her friends was at their apartment before the two of them were to go bowling, my mother and father got into an argument. My mother hit him first and he responded with a punch, fattening her lip before she could hurry out the door. He said she gave him too much mouth in front of her friends and he would not be embarrassed. She wanted to leave him, would talk about it, but she didn't know where to go. My mother spent hours flipping through the newspaper for an affordable room, but she didn't leave. She would ask herself, Why did she love him more than herself? She didn't have an answer.

She was eighteen when she became pregnant with me. She thought to herself, *I will finally have someone to love me as much as I love them.* Determined to have a safe pregnancy, my mother cut her work hours short. At five months, she stopped working altogether. She went on unemployment instead of disability, which still gave her an income. Jobless, my father told her to move back with Mrs. Hargis and she did. Feeling emotionally bound to my father, my mother kept the keys to their apartment and stopped by one day to surprise him. He was there with a girl. She was pregnant, had proof that my father was a cheater, and she still couldn't waddle away from him.

The closer she got to her due date, the more she stayed at his apartment because he was near Harlem Hospital. They were smoking a joint and watching a movie when her water broke. I arrived the next morning at 6:05 a.m.; my mother had been born at 6:05 p.m., nineteen years earlier. She believed I was meant for her. I was a pink baby who weighed a mere five pounds, fifteen ounces and had a curl in the middle of my head, which my mother had noted in her delirium. When the nurses brought the infants to the new moms to take home, they gave me to another lady. My mother knew a mistake had been made because of that curl and said, "I believe that's my baby." They checked my tag, gasped in shock, and put me in my mother's arms. She almost lost me.

From the hospital, we went to Mrs. Hargis's. My mother stayed home until the day before I turned three months and went to work at Lane Bryant's warehouse. She was in the union, making decent money, and Mrs. Hargis babysat. It was a good system that my father did not take part in, except to complain. During one visit to Mrs. Hargis, he saw I had a diaper rash and lost it. He demanded I stay with his family, whom he said knew how to raise babies, so my mother took me to his Aunt Maize's in the Bronx while she worked, seeing me only on the weekends.

When I was born, I came out with both feet facing the same direction and had corrective casts placed on my legs when I turned three months. My mother was grateful for my father's mother, who helped her soak and remove the casts every night before I went to the doctor to have them rewrapped. But when I was done with the leg bars, something horrible happened.

It was around Easter and my mother was warming my bottle in a pot on the stove. She left me on the counter between the stove and the sink while she got something out of the refrigerator. It was just a few seconds, and she was only a few steps away. I wanted that bottle so badly I reached for it. My mother turned, saw what was happening, and screamed. As a reflex, my arm fell into the boiling water. Not knowing what to do, she iced, then wrapped it. The next morning, she awoke to my arm blanketed in blisters. I went from the emergency room to the intensive care unit, with hospital officials battering my mother with questions. She pleaded with them to not take her baby, that I was all she had. She was hysterical. I stayed in the hospital for one agonizing month, and my mother visited every night after work until they kicked her out. The doctors thought my fingers would web together, that I was going to have problems bending my wrist, holding a pencil. My father threatened to take me from her, said it was my mother's fault because she was negligent. She believed him to the point of heartbreak.

Over the years she has asked herself why she was afraid to be without a man who threatened to make her motherless but then pulled her into a place where she couldn't put her child to bed or kiss her good night. Blindsided, she didn't see the pain in my eyes when we were inside the Community; she could only see her own struggles. She hated sleeping on the floor, having her underwear stolen and her shoes and coats being worn without permission. Pray five times a day, cover her face, her head, her identity. She couldn't speak to me because the children spoke only Arabic, so I couldn't translate my feelings or what I was going through. She lost two years of my life to that house because she didn't know how to say no.

When I thought back to some of the pages Ummi shared with me about her childhood, I can see her handwriting echoing my experience from a different time: *I was running down the stairs to go outside to play and bumped into my mother, who was coming up to get me. Then I remember being told by my daddy that my mother wasn't coming back.*

Thinking about Ummi at that young age, I thought maybe she did know how I felt inside the Community—the isolation, the confusion, the self-blaming. Maybe she understood what I had felt a lot better than I had ever given her credit for. I wanted that to be true.

Seven

Jumah (1979)

One Friday prayer, trouble found me. I remember the events as clearly as if I'd dreamed them last night before they dissipated like a fog. Ummi, who didn't know all the pieces, knew I remembered enough to describe an unsteady set of stairs and a dark basement in stark detail.

"Wow," she said. "If I wasn't there with you, I would have thought you were making the whole thing up."

If she hadn't confirmed it, I would have thought I made it up as well. This one event was sort of like the first time I learned to ride a bicycle without training wheels or getting lost in a theme park. On any given day in the Community, I often felt like a new swimmer sinking in an abyss, where the bottom was unseen, unfelt, unfathomable, and I was forever afraid because the surface seemed unbreakable. My loneliness was odd considering I was never alone—the Ums were always there, presenting a hardness that made me feel like a heavy load they had to heave up steep mountains and across sinking sands. The girls were there too, all limbs and soft chatter. Solitude wasn't sacred so even though I felt like nobody, I was always around another body.

Then came *jumah*, the Muslim equivalent to Christian Sundays, the day where I forgot my solitude and reveled in the Community's camaraderie. Every Friday we left behind our drab colors for a brilliant white. It was the only day of the week I felt part of something so grand it was incomprehensible to anyone who wasn't a part. On Fridays, I didn't feel I was missing what children on the outside had because I had something they didn't—a different language, a huge family, and a God so big He needed more letters. We practically glowed in our garbs.

While Sunday through Thursday I sat wondering how my parents could still be mesmerized with the Community, even after a year passed by, weeks eroding the way waves take grains of sand, I understood on Friday. At the time, my parents seemed to have a severe need for a religion, a belief system that came from people who resembled them. Being a part of the Community, they felt linked to a larger chain, connected to something bigger than ourselves, and those in the Community strongly believed we were going to make changes, create new social realities, and save our people from whatever they needed saving from.

For us girls, *jumah* was when our fathers could be seen looking like heroes, disciples of the divine and not the proselytizing incense peddlers that people on the street corners and subway trains took them for. Every Friday, I thrilled watching them in their crisp bleach-white *jalabiyas*, walking two by two across Bushwick Avenue's busy two-way strip. This was a street that cars sped down, oftentimes running lights. Sirens from fire trucks, police cruisers, and ambulances were heard constantly, zipping down the avenue at breakneck speeds because there was always someone in need of saving.

Our fathers, piously focused enough for an easy entrance into heaven, stopped traffic as they crossed the street to the *masjid* for prayer. Horns didn't blow, nor would impatient drivers yell, as they marched in rhythmic unison with high heads and ramrod backs, intent upon nothing but their destination. We, their daughters, pressed our faces against the windows to see if we could spot our protectors. Witnessing this magic, this silent control over one's environment, excited us.

Even the Ums ran to where we stood, grinning and looking out like wives waiting for husbands to return from a long-fought war. Pumping their fists in the air, the Ums would cheer, "Yeah! Look at our Brothers!" They high-fived and hip bumped each other through wide grins, the only times we saw their faces soften. We were our fathers' unseen supporters, their women were their veiled mascots, and just their simple act of walking across a crowded street in silence was enough to make us feel like we were down with the most important movement in the world. It was easy to lose ourselves in this exact moment as our pride swelled and overflowed to the brink where we could almost drown ourselves in it. As soon as the Brothers were out of sight, we quickly washed, scrubbed, and polished ourselves for prayer.

While some girls washed in the tub, I was at the sink hurriedly splashing water on my face and ears as the Ums scrutinized us, making sure no one took longer than necessary but that we were cleaning correctly. The last thing they wanted to see were dirty girls dressed in white. I slid my hijab onto my head and lined up behind the fastest washer. *Jumah* was also one of the only times I got to be in the same room with both my parents.

As much as I liked *jumah*, it was also a reminder of what my family had become—separated, rarely in the same place for long. Catching a glimpse of my father gliding across Bushwick Avenue and knowing I'd kneel on the same floor as my mother didn't erase the invisible restraints. It was a reminder of Isa's power. The man who declared himself an imam, who some people ran behind, ran after, or ran away from. The man who somehow got mothers and fathers to surrender their children for a God they had never sought before.

I saw a set of narrow spiral stairs leading down to the prayer room. Ummi said the spiral stairs I'm thinking of led somewhere else and getting to the basement was the same kind of rickety straight stairs found in any house with a basement, but even if the stairs were in the wrong place, this was how I remembered the event:

Upon getting to the prayer room, I saw the men already positioned on their knees like bent angels with their palms upturned. They were stunning in their submission, and their submission made it easier for everyone else to follow suit. Men always prayed in front of the women, and the women always prayed in front of the children, with the girls always praying behind the boys. I would wonder why we couldn't pray together when we all kneeled the same way, asked for the same love in the same language. Why were little girls so different from little boys? Why were women not able to pray next to men?

The Ums used to say the main problem with me, why I had a ruler as my namesake, was I asked too many questions. I couldn't sit and make *salat*. I wanted to know why things were done the way they were. I remember thinking how I could ask Allah for anything I wanted, but I couldn't actually have it; I could pray to be with my mother, but I was forbidden against sitting next to her. I looked around at everyone in the room, desperately seeking Ummi, but she was just one cloud in a skyful of whiteness. The room looked like an angel's convention.

"A salaam alaikum," one of the Brothers welcomed from the front of the room.

"Walaikum a salaam," the room boomed back. In unison with everyone else, I kneeled with my feet tucked under, my palms facing upward, and chin tucked into my chest.

"Allahu Akbar." The Brother's call resounded around the room.

The entire room responded, *"Allahu Akbar."* Instead of praying, I couldn't stop from thinking of my mother. I knew she was sitting in the same position, mouthing "*bismillah alrahman al rahim*" ("in the name of Allah") in a long white dress, *khimar*, and hijab. She was praying with her Sisters, and deep down to my toes, I knew that made her happy. As the prayer went on, the room turned into a wave of whispering spirits. I heard some Ums whimpering. I wondered if Ummi was one of them.

Without knowing why, my face grew hot and my eyes started to burn. I couldn't feel my feet or my knees. I tried to wipe my forehead, but my arms felt too heavy to lift. I wanted to leave. I needed Allah's help, yet He seemed to only help Imam Isa. I wanted to know for certain Allah was good, but there seemed no real way of knowing. Since Ummi wouldn't do it, I prayed for Allah to pick her up and carry both of us out of this crowded room of Arabic chants and prayer rugs. I always prayed for that.

When *jumah* ended, I rolled up my rug and looked around for Ummi. Weaving in and out of Ums and Abbus, I searched for eyes like mine. I found them next to the Brother who had conducted the prayer and was now talking to a few people. Sliding next to my mother, I yanked at her dress until she noticed me. Abbu stood on her other side but said nothing. I saw Ummi's eyes go directly to all the other eyes looking down at me.

"Is she your daughter?" the Brother asked my parents. They both said yes, and I instantly felt ashamed. To me he asked, "Why aren't you with your Ums?"

My mother grabbed my hand and squeezed it. Ummi said something in broken Arabic and English, and I could see everyone's annoyance, including my father's. "She should be with the others," my father said in fluid Arabic. Lowering her eyes, Ummi turned while holding my hand. The Ums and the girls were gone.

Stooping down, Ummi said, "You see this?" She motioned to the room with her head. "You're the only child here. Do not do this again. You hear me?" Her voice was low, but her anger ate at pieces of me. "Now get upstairs before anyone else sees you down here." She hugged me, tapped me on the butt, then walked back to the front of the room.

When I got to the stairs, Ums and Abbus were ahead of me. No one seemed to see me, and I was afraid to ask for help. I stepped to the side and closed my eyes to the soft sounds of carpet flattening and Arabic being spoken in short, fluent phrases. Of all the times I wanted to make myself invisible, I finally felt I was. When I opened my eyes, I was alone. I looked up at the stairs and sucked in enough air to fill the sky. One step at a time, I ascended.

Exhaling, I grabbed the railing. I counted to five and took another step, then another, and another. Not knowing why, I cried. I used the hand not clutching the rail to brush the tears away. Looking up, the room seemed to spin and loop in circles around me. When I was finally at the top, the door to the stairs swung open and startled me back down with the distant voice of a woman who said something in Arabic. I was in full spinning motion with my legs rotating up and over my head. I felt the vibration of feet ten times bigger than my own descend. One step at a time, without urgency.

Then I felt fingers on me. I heard, "Come. Get up, child." The Um put me on my feet. Her hijab and veil were still on, so all I saw were almond-shaped, chocolate-colored eyes. I knew them. "I was looking for your behind. What in Allah's name are you doing down here?" It was one of my Ums. She had me by my shoulders, squeezing hard. I winced; she squeezed harder. "How did you get separated from us? Wait until you get upstairs." She spun me around to climb back up again.

The journey to the room was a plank walk. My shoes echoed a click-clomp off the hardwood floor. The Um, who walked briskly in thick white socks that hugged her feet so tightly I saw the impression of her toes with every step, didn't make a sound.

Eight

The Darkest Night

I came face-to-face with a shut door whose calm interior rattled me. I turned to the Um who found me and asked for my mother.

"*Askuty!* Shut up! You know you cannot go to your mother. You know crying won't help. Now get inside." She nudged me forward. Not wanting to open my own torture chamber, I stood still. "Turn that knob before I have to."

I tried to think of an Um who had been kind to me and couldn't. Sometimes I couldn't tell one from another because they mostly spoke in short, harsh sentences with tough tones. There was not one of them who would welcome my return with a smile. Pushing me aside, the Um placed her big hand on the knob and with a flick of her wrist turned it. Before the room was in full view, I could see light. Everyone was still awake. As the door widened, the Um who would have me screaming approached.

Looking at me, she thanked the Um with the big hands. "Get your behind in this room. Now!" she ordered. I scurried across the threshold but not too far. A couple of the Ums and girls cocked their heads with questioning looks, curious as to why an Um had to fetch me with nothing on her feet but cotton that revealed the outline of her toes.

Looking down, I watched as the material between my shoulders rose and fell in staccato pulses. A giant hovering over me, the angry Um's legs easily carried her across the room in two long steps. Not many of the Ums left an individual impression on me, but this was one who made sure I paid for every transgression, so I never forgot her. Rather than look into her face, I stayed focused on the slender fingers that grew out of her knuckles. She closed the door and pulled me deeper into the room. When she spoke, it was with a voice that wasn't sharp like a dagger but blunt like a billy club. Even though the other three Ums were upset, they weren't the ones I feared.

"What did you think you were doing?" the Um asked. "Every time I turn around, you're into something and we have to bring out a ruler. Why is that?" Before I could answer, she continued, "You must like trouble. Well, let's see."

I was moving only because she was dragging me across the floor. Throwing me on my back while I squirmed at her feet, she grabbed my right foot and with her free hand yanked off my shoe and sock. Another Um handed her a ruler and in one seamless motion, the executor was in squat position on a stool, swinging her arm up over her head and bringing it down full speed across the bottom of my bare foot. Every time the wood hit, the Um spoke.

"You'll learn one day." The ruler came down on my heel and sent nettle-splintering pain through my shins. "Never met a little girl so lawless." The ruler fell again, landing on the balls of my feet.

"But I didn't mean it!" I cried.

"Still talking back?" She then swept up my left foot and pulled off the other shoe and sock. I closed my eyes.

Several more licks lashed my feet before the Um pulled me up and snatched two of my fingers open. When she swung the ruler again, I thought she might hit herself, but she was a marksman who didn't miss her target. I was so battered I thought if she opened her hands I would have slipped through her fingers onto the floor's wooden panels.

I wondered where Ummi was and how she would have felt if she knew about this beating. Knowing there were no heroes, I just wanted it to be over so I could go to sleep and forget everything. I didn't want to think about holding my screams in or begging for mercy I wasn't going to get.

When I opened my palms, the ruler came down so swift it made the sound of one handclap. Fire shot up my wrist and burned there. Reflex made me pull back and beg for my mother again, but how could I help myself? The Ums must have thought I was a brat; I felt broken. Hanging off the hinges by a small thread of hope, broken. To keep my mind off the pain, I tried to count the beats. Four, seven, ten, but even that was a waste—it was like the Um was on automatic and I hadn't learned all my numbers yet anyway. I was only about three years old. Before I understood what was happening next, the Um snatched me by the collar of my dress, pulling the seams into my armpits.

I struggled, a crocodile in a cage. I was dragged thrashing and screaming to the play yard's door. It took all four Ums to grab every flailing piece of me. Though they were stronger, they didn't attempt to subdue me but allowed me to act a fool. I imagined the other girls in the room were horrified. Since I'd been there, none of them had ever showed so much aggression toward the Ums. None of them had a ruler named after them. I was the example of what not to do if any of us had a prayer of surviving. Those girls were smarter than I was for managing to dodge the ruler-stinging assaults I somehow couldn't. Or maybe they were more afraid of the Ums than I was. There were seven of us to every one of them, and though we were only two or three years old, restlessness against one's abandonment knows no age. Similar to correction officers who work tirelessly to shock passivity into the hundreds of prisoners they patrolled, the Ums knew exactly how to grind our heavy hearts into fear.

Lugging me like a slaughtered sheep, the Ums carried me to the play yard's back door, quickly swung it open, and just as quickly threw me out. As mean and stone-faced as they were, I didn't think they meant this. After all, they were women, and women were supposed to have soft hearts for children. So I begged. Said I was afraid. Beatings were one thing, but I had never been thrown outside alone before. The evil Um seemed almost content I was regretful.

"You will sit out here and think about what you did," she said. Then the beating Um and the other three who stood behind her stepped back. They were bluffing; they couldn't be serious about leaving me out there to think. Yet it was no bluff. When I moved forward, the scary Um slammed the door shut. It click-clacked, the sound of kissing metals. The door was locked and the chain was on. Only one streetlamp lit the night. I grabbed the knob and turned it knowing it wouldn't open.

The night was so big and mysterious I couldn't face it. I was afraid of the moon overhead, spotlighting my every move. I imagined branches feet away on the sidewalk, casting leering shadows through the metal gates and into the playground, were signs of something evil. Turning back to the door, I made dull thud sounds with my fists and feet. I slammed my body against a door that stood strong and sturdy in its frame. I told myself I wouldn't stop until either the door or I collapsed. I was thinking about reaching for the window when the curtain ruffled. An Um looked out at me through the glass and shook her head. Tired, I had no choice but to sit and wait. I needed a door to open and knew I had to pray for it. At least that's what I'd heard some of the Ums say—pray, believe, and you shall receive.

I wrapped my dress around my knees and feet and brought my knees up to my chest, shivering more against the darkness than the night's air. I rocked back and forth thinking of escape. Would I have to throw myself over the barbed wire the way I dreamed? I looked around the playground, afraid something would jump out at me. The yard felt alive. Leaves rustled as the wind pushed them to the ground and branches tapped against one another. I think I started hallucinating because I swore the wooden horse I liked to ride started a silent rock.

I couldn't hear the hinges creaking or the thump of the tail hitting the matted ground when it swung backward, but I swear it moved.

I prayed. I rocked back and forth. I mouthed Ummi's name over and over as if I had seen the boogeyman and couldn't shake the image of him creeping from a closet. The longer I prayed, the more intense the sky grew. My mind had gone somewhere, and I was going with it. The sky shifted and as I said "Allah," I imagined a face looked down at me. I bit my bottom lip, did anything I could to halt the roll of new tears because I didn't want anything to hear them falling. I imagined everything could hear me, that I was a lamb left out for slaughter for the night's wolves. I called on Allah even though I wasn't sure He was real. My teeth chattered, so I bit down harder on my lip, tasting the tart iron of blood.

The horse rocked its silent rock and an amorphous face surveyed me. At least that's what my mind saw. I knew there was no way I could have fallen asleep on the steps with the night's noises whispering in my ear, yet I didn't feel alone. Jumping up, I banged on the door again. The entire neighborhood was going to hear me if need be. A man in a blue coat with a hood walked up to the gate. He watched with his fingers hooked into the metal webbings as I screamed.

I was hysterical. I pounded the door with my clenched fists and kicked at it with my bruised feet. The moon stared on my back. Looking out the window and probably seeing the man at the gate, one of the Ums came to the door. The chain clinked and the two locks reversed. Still punching and kicking when the door opened, I fell face forward into the room. Everything went black.

Nine

The Awakening

Go to the well, the voices said. Quiet, I listened. *Go to the well.* My tongue was dry, as if cotton balls rested in the roof of my mouth. I guess all the screaming took everything I had and left a drought. I saw the room luminous and bigger than it had ever appeared before. Then I was aware of soft hands with long piano fingers stroking my head. The hands were familiar, but I didn't believe. I ignored the scent, refused to let it trick me. Yet Ummi was there, looking at me with her own dark eyes and putting cool water to my lips. Where'd she come from? And did she know what happened? I didn't have it in me to ask. I was tired and finally afraid of these women and this place. I wanted out. I didn't know what I had to do, how many more of those punishments I'd have to endure before my mother came to her senses and packed me and the remnants of our lives into a neat package and got us out, with or without my father.

Rocking me close with her hurried heartbeat hammering against my chest, I let her snuggle me, rub my back, coo at me. I rested my right shoulder in the crux of her underarm. Pushed my chin deep into her chest. Ummi wrapped me in the extra material of her dress, swaddled me close. I wondered what she was thinking. Was she angry? What she was going to do, if anything, I didn't know. I knew I was done with this place. Ummi said she was sorry. She knew what happened. The Ums told her all about it, and so did the little girls who appeared shaken by the incident. Ummi said it wouldn't happen again, but how could I trust her? How could I trust them? She wasn't there when it happened the first time, and I had no faith it wouldn't happen again. I was beginning to trust no one. Not even Ummi. I felt alone and left to navigate the fear maze with the little bit of quietness I had in me. The Community seemed to want children who knew what discipline was and what it felt like, regardless of age, and I felt I had to stop fighting and learn to submit as long as I was there.

My well was dry. I had no more to give except for the simple hope, the simple wish that something would trigger my mother into wanting to leave. If it wasn't me being thrown outside, then I hoped there was something more unacceptable to make her throw her hands up and say, "We're leaving this joint." But my mother didn't say that as she cooed me awake after the beating. She just kept saying she was sorry and it wouldn't happen again. I thought how much I disliked these Ums and how they didn't seem to like Ummi. When other mothers visited, the Ums chatted them up. Told them how sweet and smart their little Latifah or Hanifah was. How disciplined and good Safara's Arabic had gotten. But not me. They gave Ummi no praiseworthy reviews about my behavior or progress. I was thinking this when Ummi bent her mouth to my ear and said, "Enough." Nothing else. She kissed my forehead and rocked me back to sleep.

When I awoke again, the mat was empty except for my balled-up body. Six eyes and three veils faced me. I instantly wondered where Ummi was and felt silly because I knew she wouldn't be there. I wondered if she had been there as I imagined, saying "Enough." Had the fingers on my head been real or another hallucination? I wanted her with me even though I knew it was forbidden. The aftereffect was fuzzy, but I remember the Ums' sarcasm.

"Ah, the princess is finally awake," an Um said.

"While everyone's been at school for the past day and a half, you've been here, sleeping, because your mother went to Isa's wife. The next thing we know, Zafirah is knocking on our door, telling us to let you sleep," the shorter Um with the gray eyes said. "We don't need Zafirah, or anyone for that matter, coming to this door asking us to spare you. From the beginning, you've been a problem. Constantly asking for your mother. Crying for your mother. Going miserable whenever she's around. I've been here for three years and Isa's wives have never come knocking asking me to spare a child. Never."

I, too, had never witnessed such a thing and somehow knew this interference from Ummi would sink me deeper into the well of scorn the Ums had already cast me into. After the speech, rather than conclude it with an arm grab or a pinch, they silently sent all their angry attention my way. For a few tense minutes, these women hovered over me falcon-like, peering with keen eyes and elbows jutting from their sides like wings. Then they sighed with annoyance, turned around, and walked away from me.

If children my age weren't being disciplined, spun dry to withstand doubtful outsiders, or instructed to learn the innuendos of Isa's Islam, it was assumed we were all right as long as we were cared for and quiet. I felt the Ums weren't speaking to me but around me; I was simply a witness to the injustice they called preferential treatment. I learned it started with Imam Isa and his wives, who lived like Allah's chosen ones in comfort and warmth, and trickled down to the *mujahids*, the guards, and their wives. The soldiers who protected us deserved respect, but that respect also came double- and triple-fold. There was a wife, maybe multiple, and wives had to be acknowledged. In addition, the master's children and those of his overseers were afforded a certain level of kindness. All Ums and Abbus knew about the favoritism bestowed on those who were not related to either Imam Isa or to a *mujahid* but who received leniency because they were friends of one or both. I imagined it was the ones in the inner circle the Ums disliked the most. The men or women who moved no mountains, taught no Arabic, nor could recite passages from the Qur'an yet who received provisions some only wished for. That was probably what fueled their resentment against Ummi and ultimately me.

It didn't help that I constantly asked for her, which made me appear spoiled. Maybe I was. The wooden handclaps didn't deaden the justification I felt in wanting Ummi. The wooden handclaps also didn't steady the unshaken resentment growing inside me toward Ummi. I believed she knew my caregivers were women who used exile as an acceptable form of punishment for a three-year-old and did nothing about it. I wondered if she knew but then thought these were women with children of their own. Surely no one imagined they would hurt us.

When the Ums decided I had lain around long enough, it was time to wash my day-old stink and return to the order of things. As I sloughed away nightmares of dark clouds and the resounding echoes of wood to flesh, I realized I was upset with Ummi for tattling and for not handling the Ums herself. I wondered why she wouldn't use her own voice. Once dressed, I went into the yard with the other kids but had no desire to play. My body was sore and my feet still throbbed. The back of my throat clawed, and everything inside me felt ball-and-chain heavy. Even when some of my mates tried to bring me into a seesaw share, I declined, feeling my stomach lurch at the image of my feet lifting off the ground. I wanted to know where Ummi was and what had to happen.

While the expulsion was the first and last time I was kicked out, the ruler remained a regular regulator. Hands and feet were favorite whacking spots because the Ums said blood rose quicker there, which meant it hurt more. This was true. Several times I couldn't hold a pencil in class because my hands were too swollen.

~

Years after we left and I asked my father how Grandma felt about us being in the Community, he said she liked that it gave us purpose and would go down to the mosque herself at times and take lessons. I wondered if she knew about the beatings. The irony was when we finally left, my grandmother would say, "Stop talking all this Muslim, Arabic nonsense," when I said my dinner prayers. Another time she told me, "I would tell your mother, 'Look at my granddaughter, dressed like some third-world child. Why are you doing this? If you two want to put yourselves through this, fine, but why must Nicky be punished?'"

I have lost many details of the beatings I received while inside the Community, but I remember plenty of body-sore sleeps as sometimes the Ums lined us up to receive rulers, a quick hand to the mouth following a smart comment, being pulled across the blue mat and it making a *tchhhhhh* sound, as well as facing threats of being locked outside again. Maybe the Ums did throw me out again, but once was enough for me to remember so that was all I stored. Maybe I found it too difficult to reconcile adults, like my grandmother, knowing something was off-track and still not stepping in.

I believed Grandma supported my father—that was her job—yet during my childhood when I spent most of my Christmases with her, she defied my parents' wishes by offering Sulaiman and me anything she knew to be forbidden. "Just a little taste. I won't tell your parents," Grandma would say about pork. Then more boldly, she'd dress us in the Sunday best she had bought and stashed away for our visits and drag us to her small white church up the block on 103rd Street and First Avenue to pray, read from the Bible, and mumble gospel hymns while clapping our hands to the rhythm of the choir.

Just as my memories don't always jibe with my parents', theirs are just as selective. Throughout the years I have asked Ummi in various ways if she knew about the tension between the Ums and me, and she always gave a different response. Once she said she didn't know what I was talking about; she'd never heard about abuse. Another time she said there were rumors some of the children were being beaten by their Ums, which is why she kept a close eye on me. Then one day she said she heard about my beatings specifically, heard I talked too much and asked too many questions about seeing her and it infuriated the Ums, but she hadn't heard that I was ever thrown outside. Finally, she admitted she knew I was put out as punishment but that it wasn't long; it was meant to tease a smidgen of fear into me. She also said we left because of the abuse, that she learned the Ums discarded me like a trash bag, but I eventually discovered that was only a piece of it.

My father, on the other hand, seemed oblivious. He once said he thought I didn't speak because I was angry with him; Ummi would've told him if something was wrong. He tried to assure me. "We would've been out of there so fast and I would've turned that place upside down had I known you were being beaten."

Maybe he would've. Or maybe Ummi did tell him, and years of guilt obliterated the memory.

Ten

Grandma

I don't know why Grandma visited, because there were hardly ever any celebrations. Birthdays, anniversaries, and national celebrations were nonexistent in the Community. We didn't observe New Year's, Thanksgiving, the Fourth of July, or Mother's Day, to name the big ones. The only event we observed with a bang—something worth blowing whistles, ringing bells, and eating real food for—was Eid al-Fitr, the three-day celebration that marked the ending of the monthlong holy fast of Ramadan. I was taught a Muslim wasn't a Muslim unless he observed Ramadan, a purification sacrifice to Allah. Like Lent to Catholics or Yom Kippur for Jews, Ramadan was supposed to bring a Muslim closer to spiritual atonement. It was one of the five pillars of faith that even some of the most undevout Muslims practiced, abstaining from food and water, from sunup to sundown, to quietly reflect instead.

Imam Isa said vanity was the problem and his version of Islam, with its strict rules and bare-bones living policy, was the solution. It was vanity that made people want to show off and vanity that caused a man to beg or steal. By arguing against individualism, excessive freedoms, and desires, Imam Isa diminished the need for special personal days. As a result, I didn't think about my birthday, didn't know when it was, and understood it didn't matter. My aging a year was little significance to the work that needed to be done inside and outside the Community's codes. We were looking at a new decade, America was about to elect a new president whose trickle-down policies would make the poor poorer, and those in the Community felt infiltrated and spied on by government eyes. A personal celebration was the last thing they thought about.

When Ummi told me Abbu and Grandma were visiting, I wanted it to have something to do with my recent beating. That I was being rescued in some way. There was no calendar in my room, just a clock, and the days clicked by without any concrete meaning, which meant it could have easily been my birthday or the New Year and I wouldn't have known. Not knowing the reason for my grandmother's visit was a point of false hope. Life on the outside didn't exist until people on the outside reminded us of everything we'd left behind that we remembered. This was why my grandmother's visit excited and mystified me; I felt there was purpose to her presence.

My grandmother was born in the middle of the Depression in New York City and belonged to a family of seven. Her father emigrated from Barbados when he was eighteen. His grainy black-and-white passport photo showed a thin young man with sharp bone structure and brown almond eyes, his hair cut low over a smooth, high forehead and straight nose. My grandmother's mother was from Charleston, South Carolina. These two raised my grandmother Dorothy, who was a young girl during the Second World War and came of age in the 1950s when everyone in America was afraid of communism or anything not American. Between the Korean War, the Cuban Revolution, and countries like Sierra Leone, Nigeria, and Ghana digging deep into their wombs to start the tireless work of thawing off centuries of colonization when she came of age, my grandmother was weary of political unrest and sought agreement with the Black Christian churches who said we had to be consciously smarter than the rest. I didn't think she understood anything about being a Black Muslim.

I didn't know how Grandma felt, but I anticipated the visit. When Ummi came to my room, she seemed nervous and fidgeted with the front of my hijab until it was just right. I thought my grandmother would sit with me in the room the way my mother did until Ummi explained no one was allowed in the house unless they lived, worked, or got a pass to be there.

Quietly, she whispered reminders. "Try to look as happy as you can when you see Grandma. Smile for her. Give her a hug and a kiss. Try to talk to her a little."

With a kiss, she left me to my group and to the Ums, who took a small cluster of us downstairs single file. Outside, trees rested their roots in dry ground, and the air smelled crisp and cool. My mother and father stood with my grandmother and another older woman. Grandma was no taller than five foot three in size 6 heels and a pillbox fox hat that complemented her round eyes, wispy, gray-flecked hair, and skin the color of cooked caramel. Her petite frame was a distraction to the bad-to-the-bone kind of woman she was, which was someone who had no qualms saying what was going on beneath that dead fox of hers.

What I remembered most about the woman with Grandma was her eyes looked as tired as my grandmother's. I hadn't been seen yet, so I stood there studying everyone. I couldn't hear their voices, but I imagined what they said. Their bodies and faces gave them away. Grandma told them, "Look at you two," because she would have. My parents responded with kisses on her cheeks.

Next, there was small talk before specific talk followed by angry talk. I saw my parents tense up, grow irritated, and my father threw a small tantrum. My grandmother apologized and my mother thought them both insane.

"Papa, you look good," Grandma said. "They treating you all right in here?"

"Yes, Ma," my father replied.

If I could have read my mother's thoughts the way I did her body language, she was thinking, *The man is twenty-four years old, married with a child, and his mother is still wiping sweat from his brow.* Ummi's face was covered, but her eyes glared at both my father and grandmother. Knowing my grandmother, she got right to her feelings.

"You know I don't like you in this place, James."

"How many times do I have to tell you, Ma? It's Azim, for goodness' sake, not James. Okay?"

"Okay, I'm sorry, but you were my son first and I named you James. All this other stuff, this dressing like you're some crazy Arab and speaking some funny language, I didn't teach you any of that."

"Look. I'm a Muslim, and I'm not trying to be anything but what I am."

Scared of his anger, Grandma took a step back and allowed my father room to speak.

"Now, if you came here to get on my nerves and make me mad, which is what you're doing, then you can go back home. I have enough to deal with."

If my father never felt proud about anything in his life, I knew he did as a Muslim. I knew he felt like part of a clan of original men. Men whose fathers' fathers fathered ancient history. In the Community, he was looked at as a person with a purpose. If he one day wanted to devote himself to becoming an imam, he could, and if he wanted to take up arms, no one would have told him he didn't have the right to defend his family or his brethren. He walked with his head high and his shoulders squared against naysayers. He was not a man-child but a sphinx in the making, and I believed he never felt anything as powerful before in his life, not even as Papa in his own family. When he expressed his exasperation to my grandmother, I'm sure he meant it. Never again would he feel his feelings were invalid. The Community was making him a man. It appeared my grandmother understood and offered an olive branch of a smile.

"I'm sorry. I don't mean to upset you," Grandma said. "I just want to make sure you two are all right." Then turning to Ummi, the little lady with the razor-sharp questions softened up for my mother.

"I'm great, Ma. How are you?"

"You sure you okay? You look like you losing more weight, and Lord knows you can't afford to."

Then Grandma grabbed a handful of my mother's dress and pulled it snugly around her slight frame.

"See? Look like you starving under all this material."

"Ma, I'm fine. Really."

"Well, you don't look fine."

My mother didn't respond but quietly exhaled and looked around. She spotted me first; then my father did, followed by my grandmother.

I forced my feet forward and stood shyly in front of them. My grandmother gasped at how big I was getting. My mother scooped me up for my grandmother to throw her arms around me; the closeness of Ummi's breath, her strong arms supporting my bottom, and her neck straining forward against my arms felt like another life. I wasn't in her arms long before her eyes shifted to a place behind me where my Ums stood watching. As soon as Ummi put me down, my grandmother pulled me toward her and said she loved me. As if she'd forgotten something, she whirled around to the smiling woman next to her and said, "This is your father's godmother. She has grandkids here, too, but she wanted to see you."

It was then I understood why the woman's eyes looked like my grandmother's. She, too, had little people behind these doors. My father's godmother commented on how sad I looked and then started off to see her own sad-eyed kin. Stopping the round woman before she could leave, my father kissed her on both cheeks and said he had to go back to work.

To Grandma he said, "I'll call you later, Ma, to make sure you got home okay."

"But we just got here," Grandma protested.

Kissing my grandmother, my father said, "I understand, but I have things to do."

Grandma protested a bit more, saying she didn't see him often, but my father shut her down. When he was done reminding everyone it wasn't her choice, he was gone in five huge strides. I remember looking at my mother and seeing something change in her eyes. I couldn't tell if she was angry or sad, because although her eyes were glossy, they were tearless and her body was stiff.

The only boy in the family, my father had carte blanche when it came to my grandmother. He would complain, roll his eyes, suck his teeth, talk back, and she never seemed to get genuinely upset; she never one-upped him to show she was more powerful. Grandma hesitated to upset my father, and I believed he knew this.

My grandmother birthed five children—Lu, my father, Genie, Love, and Cookie in that order—and the only sister who liked my father was Cookie, his junior by fifteen years. When she and I got older, she told me she loved my parents so much when she was younger, she wanted to move into the place of gates and guards, kids, *khimars*, and chaos to be closer to them. I laughed and told her there was no way to get close to anything inside the Community except with one's own thoughts. I learned my parents were a paradox to many people, who thought they were either crazy or cool for making such drastic changes in their lives. I always got the feeling my grandmother thought my Community-loving parents were simply crazy.

As soon as my father left, leaving behind the sweet scent of sandalwood and myrrh, all eyes turned to me. My grandmother asked a roll call of questions, never waiting for responses. I mostly bit down on my tongue, looked far off, and shook or nodded my head. Frustrated, Grandma looked at me with wrinkled brows and narrowed eyes. Her mouth worked.

"Are you hungry?"

"Do you know your name?"

"Do you know how old you are?"

"Do you know who I am?"

"So, you remember me?"

"Then why won't you stop nodding and speak?"

"Why won't you speak to me?"

She turned her anger on my mother when I answered *naeam* or *laa*, yes or no, or didn't answer at all. I was quietly hoping my grandmother's pot would boil over so violently it would splash some common sense into the psyche of Ummi and force her to pack the remainder of her parenting skills and get me out of there. It almost worked. Grandma's last two questions required more than I could give with a couple of head movements, and this made her livid. She glared at my Ums. Stared at Ummi with eyes that no longer recognized her. I think she called Ummi unfair and asked how they could continue this life when I had become a child she no longer knew. She suggested they leave, the sooner the better, for my well-being. I was hoping Grandma would say enough and tell me let's go, but she didn't offer herself as my escape portal. That's when I knew my rescue was as dead as the animal she now clutched in her hands.

Standing in front of my grandmother and mother, my hopes evaporated and rendered me speechless. I felt adults were not to be trusted no matter how gentle their words and sympathetic their eyes. If I was able to remember who I was before the Community, I might have thrown myself at my grandmother's feet. But I was no longer that girl. Breaking the spell and her assault of questions, Grandma straightened and asked, "What's wrong with this child? What happened to my granddaughter?"

It was then I noticed the air's electricity. I could feel the Ums' defiance. See how they looked at my grandmother with a gaze that said, *We are right*. To me, one of the Ums said loudly in Arabic, "Go play with the kids." Looking at the Um who rested both hands on her wide hips, my grandmother knew I had been told to leave. She didn't have to speak Arabic to understand this show of power, and it made Grandma so angry she hit the sky about how she couldn't believe they were ruining her time with her granddaughter and she had just gotten there and had rights as a grandmother. Her face contorted and she demanded from Ummi and the Ums some answers.

"What kind of place is this?" Grandma asked. She looked as if someone had told her I wasn't her grandchild, that she had the wrong family. Adding one more bead to her string of fury, Grandma asked the question I knew she wanted to ask since her son said he was moving in.

"Who do you people think you are? This is *my* family."

Such intense emotions were rarely exhibited in the Community. We were stoic soldiers trained to keep our feelings in check and to stay in our prescribed lanes. People didn't publicly question or make demands. My mother started twisting her dress; some of the Ums' eyes grew wider while some narrowed further.

One look at my grandmother and Ummi and I saw I had to leave. The playground wasn't a courtroom, and no cases with a judge and jury were going to be heard. Rather than run around as other kids did, I claimed a spot on the sidelines. Watching the kids twirl in circles, chasing each other the way a cat chases its tail, I didn't understand their abandoned joy. How they had fun when we couldn't play when we wanted, and when we didn't want to play, we were told to do so. I didn't feel like a child in the Community but instead felt like a tiny adult given an advanced placement course on the science of struggle.

Eventually Grandma called me back. The woman who wore my grandmother's eyes returned. I tried to read everyone's faces to see if I should take my mother's hand and turn on my heels before anyone changed their minds, but when I looked closely, I saw I wasn't leaving. Then my grandmother spoke.

"I know you know who I am, and I know you understand me, don't you?"

I nodded my head yes. It seemed most important to Grandma that I knew who she was and what she was saying. She looked up and pointed to the clouds.

"We never know what God or Allah or whomever they teach you in here that God is has in store for us, but He loves you and loves you better than anyone can," she preached. "Remember that. As long as I have breath in my body and you're still here, I'm coming to visit. I don't care what those—"

I cannot recall what was said after that.

Eleven

Jihad: Ummi's Reveal

It was 2010 and I was sitting in my mother's kitchen, looking out the window at barren treetops, empty rooftops, and the jagged tips of the Manhattan winter skyline. We were talking about the Community, just talking, no recording. I told her how the entire experience—abandoning who we were for a new home, names, beliefs, and twists of the tongue—were all extreme to me, including my idea of an escape, which was to throw myself over the barbed wire that surrounded our playground. My desire to leave never felt like an itch, because it was always there, pulsing from the moment I was shown a room filled with little girls and watched Ummi cross the threshold into an alternate, forbidden universe. So when I asked if she'd ever felt an itch to leave, I remember wanting her to say it had everything to do with me but laughing at myself before she could answer. I had a feeling that just as our walking into the Community had nothing to do with me, neither did leaving it.

"Did I ever have an itch? To leave?" Ummi repeated. "Many times. But I would talk myself out of that thinking."

I could tell she felt the ghost of guilt hovering by the way she closed her eyes against the question. For three decades, since she was twenty-one, Ummi's been dragging this emotional cross and remarkably has not tried to run from it. She still carried the Community's identification card, showing a solemn and serious-looking young woman draped in black cotton fabric, as a reminder of who she used to be. Chewing thoughtfully on a sandwich, I felt comfortable discussing the Community because we had been doing so for a couple of months. Ummi, however, didn't always seem comfortable with the questions, and on that cold afternoon, as I continued to inquire about her life inside the Community, I remember she closed her mouth and shut her eyes. I picked at my sandwich—various kinds of cheeses smashed between lettuce, tomatoes, and mayo—then put it down. I took a sip of water instead. Ummi's long hair, lightly traced with gray, was pulled back in a ponytail, revealing a pained look on her face. She shook her head. Said something about not being a fan of cheese because of how it smelled, which reminded her in some way of the Community.

"I'm not sure exactly when I started to change. I don't know if there was a specific thing or incident that pushed me; I just knew as time went on, I had a lot of self-doubt and anger," she said. She opened her eyes. "The more I looked at you, the less I saw my husband, the worse I felt. For good or bad, some of the other Sisters felt the same and we stuck together in misery. I walked into the Community's dos and don'ts with my heart open, and I didn't want bitterness or fear to cloud that. I made a decision and probably out of pride and stubbornness, I tried to stick to it. Plus, it wasn't always bad."

"No?" I asked.

"No, that was the magic," Ummi said, smiling. She stuck her fork into the creaminess of her potato salad, and the scent of garlic invaded the air. "For example, Friday was the best day of the week. I swelled up with so much love for my people and what we could create and maintain without outside forces, it almost tasted like homemade pound cake. We were our own leaders, teachers, and tailors. Even those we called *kafirs*, the nonbelievers, knew not to mess with us. *Jumah* was our day to show out, and the Brothers did. Seeing how they moved under the eyes of strangers who followed their every step kept us Sisters going. We loved how dignified they looked, like lions that knew they owned the earth beneath their feet, lions that took so much pride in their pride they couldn't trip up. As their women, this was all we needed to see sometimes to be reminded that every last one of us were warriors."

Her face grew sad then, as if remembering she had lost something valuable all those years ago. "Yet when *jumah* ended," Ummi continued, "I felt we went back to being the wives, the Sisters, the women who were not as important as the men and never would be. Strange things like that pendulum feeling made us huddle with and speak to Sisters we may not otherwise have spoken to."

"What do you mean?" I asked.

"There were women I knew I wouldn't have been friends with on the outside," Ummi said. "In the Community, appearances, money, how pretty your hair was, or how well you danced didn't matter. There was no other place where I could have been around so many intelligent and beautiful Black women as I was in the Community. There were women who spoke fluent Arabic and had been academics and Sisters who lovingly assisted newcomers with prayers and *wudhu*, spending hours and days of their lives to make another comfortable."

"Did you feel comfortable?" I asked her. Her eyes darted from her potato salad to my face with a look of shock. I felt I had misspoken, sounded too accusatory.

"People questioned the Community and the sacrifices we made, and I ask, How many Black folks in America could speak another language then?" Ummi said. "Or had children who went to Arabic school? Children who were proud of themselves because they were taught that they were special? How many of us grew up feeling special?"

The questions felt pointed, as if she were asking them directly of me and indirectly asking, How do you think you got so smart? Didn't I feel special because of that environment and those experiences? Didn't I know how unique it was to constantly be surrounded by Black beauty? Did I not understand the sacrifice?

"You want to know what I loved about the Community, Jamiyla, then let me tell you," Ummi said. I motioned with my hands that the floor was hers.

"Inside the Community, we weren't always on the same page, but I felt we were united in knowing we would have done what was needed for anyone there if push came to shove," Ummi said. "If one sacrificed, we all sacrificed. If a Sister was new and had nowhere to sleep, we found a way to make sure she had more than a hardwood floor beneath her. It may not have been what she was used to, but no one denied we pushed each other to be the very best women we could have been." Ummi paused, as if remembering something.

The way I felt about this sacrifice was that it was unfair to the children. Why were we turned into little soldiers because our parents wanted to become warriors? I had thoughts I felt I couldn't, at that time, share because I wanted Ummi to keep speaking, but I was pessimistic at how the women of the Community made each other better. Did those mothers not miss their children? Hadn't Ummi told me about cold showers, hardwood floors, mice in kitchen cabinets, and stolen checks and shoes? I thought she was being nostalgic.

"You feel that way even though you had to hide underwear from each other?" I asked.

"Remember, Jamiyla, I grew up as an only child who always wanted siblings. So these women became my sisters," Ummi continued. "We fought and disagreed and sometimes didn't speak, but isn't that how families are sometimes? Siblings aren't always tight. But that tension, that push-and-pull, was how it was with our Sisterhood. Everyone was important to the movement—like a link in a chain, no one could break or we'd all fall apart."

"Something happened, right?" I asked.

"Some things happened," Ummi said. "I started to feel a little broken and worked hard to psych myself up every day. Between being lonely, hungry, and sometimes very afraid of what would happen to all of us, I was jittery. And then you wouldn't talk to me. I didn't know how to fix your silence, because you weren't a quiet child before. I thought you'd outgrow it. Your silence hurt me."

A tear rolled down her left cheek. Ummi grabbed my hand and squeezed it. I squeezed back, letting my own tears fall. The sandwich and potato salad both sat untouched. We had never discussed my self-imposed childhood silence before, and I noticed she didn't ask for an explanation either. She knew I had become a replica of the girl she had been with Granny when we were inside the Community, but she didn't seem to know why.

"Do you want to know why I went quiet, Ummi?" I asked.

"You were angry with us," she said.

"No, it was as simple as language for me," I explained. "The rules were that English was forbidden, but your Arabic was limited, and you wouldn't speak English to me instead. You wanted to follow the rules. Knowing this, I decided if I couldn't express myself as I wanted to, then I would say nothing."

"You were on strike?" Ummi asked, laughing.

"No," I said. "I was afraid to get us in trouble and really didn't know another way to speak to you. I was petulant with the Ums, never with you. I was happy every time I saw you."

Ummi smiled weakly and seemed to be back in the Community. Back to wondering how long I would stay mute. Back to devising new ways to see me, whether it was through a job in the Children's House or by sneaking around. Back to rocking me to sleep in her arms so that her heartbeat was the last one I felt when dozing.

"I'm sorry," Ummi said. "I hurt that you hurt."

I was going to say that it was okay, but I didn't get it out. What Ummi said next quieted me.

"I knew from seeing how you changed that I didn't want to have another child inside," she said. "I couldn't bear the idea of giving birth to a baby, then giving him up to only see him to nurse. I couldn't accept having my son giggling, playing, and drooling on other women who didn't go through the journey of carrying him for nine months, doubling over with contractions, and twelve-plus hours of labor pains. I wasn't going to push him into a world I didn't know how to defend myself from yet. It was bad enough I lost you in the Community. I wasn't sacrificing another child." She wiped at a tear.

"Wow," I said, unable to keep my surprise to myself. The tone deafness of Ummi's statement struck me hard. It was one thing for me to have felt like a sacrifice for a belief, a desire, a vision, and another to hear the person who sacrificed me admit it. I felt a wave of confirmation roll over me that my brother had dodged a religious bullet, as I had long thought. New to my understanding, the dodge was intentional. My heart began to beat a little faster and my stomach twisted. While Ummi took me into the Community with intention and purpose, she summoned the same energy into making sure Sulaiman was never there. Ummi was looking off, somewhere far. She hadn't heard my "wow" or the indignation I exhaled.

"I would get on my knees and submit everything within me. Eventually I felt the shift," she said. "That intense desire to not raise another child there was like a half-blind person being able to see writing after years of darkness. In the beginning I used to look at the Sisters who had babies there and I envied them. I admired the courage it took to create such disciplined and amazing children from day one. Their children's first words would either be Ummi or Abbu. Being genuine Muslims was something I thought I wanted for my family, until I realized I didn't. Or rather, I knew I didn't want to be that kind of Muslim."

I didn't know what kind of Muslim Ummi thought the Community would make her, but I imagined she thought it would help strengthen her family, make her husband a focused father, a more humbled better half. Instead, my father leaned into the patriarchal, self-pleasing parts of Islam that Ummi wasn't interested in. I thought about the teenage girl whom I had interviewed after York's arrest in 2002, and her statement about adults and parents, how selfish they can be, and I still agreed. My parents and others within the Community forgot that in their quest for knowledge, guidance, a community, they sacrificed a child or children in the process.

"I was sitting on the threshold of an internal war, and this was a first for me and the Community," Ummi said. "Isa and his imams taught us one of the most important things a Muslim ever had to overcome was jihad—a holy war. After studying, asking, and listening, I understood jihad wasn't a physical war but a spiritual one with oneself."

Ummi looked at me. "Transformation had to be made and demons defeated for jihad to happen," she said. "Isa's books taught that every good Muslim came out of it with a clearer vision of one's spiritual purpose. Looking back, I was having one. At the time, I just wasn't sure if I would come out as victor or victim."

She abruptly rose from the table, disappeared, and returned with two old passports. Turning to the photo pages of each, she put her fingers on our heads. The expressions that stared back from the black-and-white pictures were blank. Ummi was stoic in a white top, her long, thick hair pulled back from her face to reveal small horseshoe-shaped earrings. I was also wearing a white top, but the large, dark eyes that sat below a row of cornrows seemed to reveal disobedience.

"Our first passport photos and we look like we'd been stunned," Ummi said with a laugh.

"We had," I said, shaking my head. She put the surprisingly new-looking passports down and rewound the clock to early 1980, when she'd met another young mother named Kalila. Months later when I recalled Kalila's story, I remembered an intense battle that gave Ummi a window into an open portal beyond the gates, but I was wrong.

When Ummi first saw Kalila in the Community—round faced; short, strong legs; with a son who was born the day before I was—she saw a possible friend. Kalila came in without a husband, leaving her big family behind in Trenton. She had heard about the mosque from a Brother who had been selling incense and books on the street. He told her about a place where her son Sharif would be guarded from dope fiends, poverty, and pistols. She was only nineteen but determined. When Ummi spoke, Kalila would look at her the way one might look at a prophet. The closeness of my and Sharif's birth dates bonded the mothers, and Ummi became Kalila's older sister. Without trying, they clicked the way two magnets do when placed near each other.

As Ummi showed her around, she hid the frustration, resentment, and sadness she felt for the Community behind her *khimar* the same way she hid her underwear and socks in her cubby. Ummi didn't want Kalila to think she couldn't bear the heavy stars and crescent moon because though there were no crosses, they did have choices. Ummi's job was to convince Kalila that she made the right one.

"She and I stayed in the same room and talked about our children for hours," Ummi remembered. "When we felt heart heavy, we went to each other for a smile or a good laugh. Whenever she needed advice, she asked me for it. When she prayed, we prayed together. Kalila followed no one or anything but her own heart. She wasn't afraid to speak her mind or wear her feelings. I knew, like me, she was trying to prove something to herself. She, too, wanted a different life, and if that meant making *salat* five times a day and covering up, so be it."

Done with lunch, Ummi automatically rose, emptied the plates, and placed them in the sink to wash. I've rarely ever seen her let dirty dishes lie. She was wearing a sleeveless blue cotton lounge dress and white flip-flops. With the sound of splashing water in the metal sink drowning out our quiet, Ummi seemed to have found her comfort zone. Back turned, hands in sudsy dishes as she methodically sponged them clean, she seemed looser when not looking at me. Less retrained, as though she could just tell a story. Her voice rose over the running water.

"When we first went to the Community, I didn't think I'd survive a night, let alone a month, but a year and a half and I was still a dedicated Um," Ummi said with a stamp of a foot. "I told Kalila how tight the Community was and how the sense of unity was the most beautiful thing I ever encountered. When she told me she didn't like being separated from her son, I let her know I went through the same emotions at first. That I spied on you every chance I got because I started hearing some children were being abused by their Ums. But I didn't think this was happening to you because I was close by. I was working in the Children's House, sometimes right downstairs or upstairs from where you were, and banked on my presence being enough to protect you." Ummi sighed. "The Community was a spiritual jungle, but I kept negative images away from Kalila. When she doubted that she could endure, I'd remind her of the struggle, the cause, the reason she came in the first place. Before Kalila got there, I had very few Sisters I could confide in. There were countless nights I talked to myself, cooed to the babies or to you, even though you were mute with me. It helped whenever we could bring Sharif and you together. I wanted to be an example of how to keep steady. Being her mentor helped remind me of the good I sought. Kalila felt like my missing screw."

Ummi wiped her hands dry on a cloth and started for the living room, her indication for me to follow. We sat on the dark brown leather sofa, sinking into its soft seats, and she instantly reached for the remote and turned on the muted television. I didn't protest but asked, "So what happened?"

Ummi was looking at the soundless television. I was looking at the multicolored socks on my feet that were placed squarely on the floor. My hands were in my lap. "There were no forces I saw that secretly worked to pull us apart. It was all Kalila," she said. "She had been there for several months, maybe not even half a year, when she packed all of her belongings and walked toward the stairs that led to the door. When I confronted her, she said she was leaving. She couldn't do it anymore. I was stunned. Most of my time in the Community was spent talking to the *tifl*. They were the only ones who seemed to understand. Now I had someone I could trust, and just like that, she was walking out." Ummi snapped her fingers.

"I asked her, 'What do you mean you're leaving? You just got here,'" Ummi said. "Kalila explained that she'd been there for weeks and wasn't happy. She didn't want to sleep on the floor, wonder if her stuff would be there when she awoke, or make appointments to see her child. I told her I'd been there for over a year and it just took some getting used to, but we learn to manage. I remember her zeroing in on that one phrase. 'Learn to manage.'" Ummi let out a sour-sounding chuckle.

"And as if I said what she was waiting for, Kalila pulled her veil down so I could clearly see her face and explained how she came to the Community, left her home and family, yet was poorer than she had ever been. She said she came because she thought she found a safe, smart place. A place where she could learn things the world didn't want us to know. She reminded me it was 1980, an entirely new decade, but we were starving while everyone else was eating. She did not appreciate the Community's power structures. I remember the resolve in her eyes, but I had my own resolution."

I was transfixed by the story of Ummi and Kalila, whom I grew up thinking of as best friends, Sharif as an annoying half cousin. I had never heard how they met or how Kalila had walked out on Ummi, taking a piece of my mother with her. On that sofa, I leaned into Ummi, trying to visualize these two young mothers negotiating their freedom with each other. One tall and wiry, weighed down from months in the Community; the other clear-eyed and big chested, uplifted by the knowledge that her family couldn't wait for her return. As Ummi spoke, I leaned so closely into her that she leaned back. I felt if I got close enough to her, her memory could transport me to the house, to the room that she and Kalila were in. I was unfamiliar with the Ummi my mother was describing, and she seemed to sense it. She shifted in her seat to face me and tucked a knee under herself.

When I reimagined their confrontation months later, I created an epic showdown that turned Ummi into a formidable, unbending palm tree. Even though Kalila was shorter and three years younger than Ummi, she was stockier. Ummi said she remembered Kalila having strong mason's hands. Sizing Kalila up, as well as her own advantages, I see Ummi brace herself. She tells Kalila she would never intentionally try to hurt her; she just wasn't going to make it easy for her to leave.

"There was an odd ritual we women had, that when one Sister left, the Sister closest to her would physically try to stop her," Ummi said. My mouth flew open. "Yes, I'd seen this happen many times." Badly wanting my mother to have been one of those fighting women, the kind of woman I had never seen in her, I imagined she somehow transformed, stood taller and bolder, and then tackled.

Kalila went for a box and Ummi threw herself at her feet, bringing Kalila and her box down. Kalila struggled to get Ummi off her. She asked why they didn't leave together. She knew Ummi wasn't happy and told her she had always seen through the warrior's mask. Ummi said it wasn't as easy for her. Kalila had an entire family. Ummi had no one. She needed Kalila to understand she couldn't leave her.

When Kalila tried to make her exit again, Ummi snatched the box from her and stood in front of the stairs. Kalila begged her to not fight her, but those bets were off. Hot-peppered fear and the taste of betrayal sat on Ummi's top lip in small sweat beads. She was shaking with adrenaline. Kalila begged, please don't make it harder than it already was, but Ummi said she couldn't do that. Placing the box on the floor, Ummi told Kalila she wasn't going to passively stand there and be abandoned. Because neither of them wanted to give in, they tussled and wrestled, screamed and cried until they were half-dead from exhaustion. When Kalila thought Ummi had had enough, she tried rationalizing.

She made another attempt to pick up the box and head for the door, and again, Ummi threw herself at her, fighting until they both realized there would be no victor. When they finally stopped, their garbs were torn and their hair stood up electrified. Kalila had small red welts on her face from where Ummi accidentally scratched her. Ummi's lips felt swollen. They sat there for a moment, drenched in sweat and breathing like they had run laps.

Kalila got up wearily and replaced the fallen items in her box. She continued to make her way down the stairs. Ummi scrambled back to her feet, both of them stumbling as if in water. From Kalila tripping down the stairs to Ummi chasing her, Kalila swinging the door open to reveal piercing daylight to Ummi tackling her again, I imagine they looked like a tumbleweed of discarded fabric. By this time they were outside, and Ummi felt as though she were losing an appendage. Her right hand. Her left foot. Ummi begged one last time, screamed at Kalila. Devastated. Kalila stopped and wrote her information on a piece of paper. She told Ummi she was sorry for not being as strong as she was.

When Ummi finished her story about Kalila, I was in tears. I hadn't known how lonely my mother was inside; I couldn't see it. I thought I had been the only one who fought to keep a piece of herself while losing everything. I felt ashamed of the many times I thought of my mother as a sadist, a misery-seeker. I was crying and sweating through my shirt. My skirt was sticking to the sofa. I grabbed Ummi's hand and held it. She wiped at my tears with her free hand.

"That Kalila was something," Ummi said. "She took her beautiful round face and ripped clothing and walked unsteadily to the pay phone across the street. I wanted so badly to leave with her, but unable to move, I sat on the steps of the Sisters' Quarters and cried for hours into the night. Aaliyah half dragged me upstairs, the crumpled paper still in my hand, and told everyone I was ill. I didn't know how I could recover, but Kalila's courage of being able to come, then go, regardless of what someone else wanted, got me to start thinking differently."

Twelve

Eye-Openers (1980)

Freedom and confinement were two things I thought I alone fought for and against. From the moment we entered the Community, with me gripping Ummi's hand, my stomach ached with an unidentifiable nervousness. I couldn't tell if the nervousness was a claustrophobic response to too many bodies under one roof or to the cacophonous sounds of a community bursting with the longing of an ancient memory of power. I was a lonely child inside the Community, but I wasn't the only one. Like the girls in the room with me, I knew that worse than being alone was once having had a mother and then losing her. I didn't have siblings divided among rooms and Ums, but I did have a desire to reclaim my mother.

After Um Kalila left, Ummi steeped in a deep sea of lonesomeness. Knowing from past heartbreaks what that abyss felt like, it was no longer difficult for her to recognize the same loneliness in my eyes. I had become so quiet my Ummi started asking if I knew who she was. As constant reflections of one another, my relentless sadness forced her to notice changes in her own behavior, in others, and compelled her to take an unbiased look at the place where she'd entrusted me.

Though Ummi obeyed, she was never comfortable with the Community's totalitarian society. Dependency was not a friend for her to lean on, but she also took pride in her dedication. It wasn't until she was past the newlywed stage and more than a year into the marriage when she started questioning how the Community could care for so many men, women, and children. Before, she didn't question why every woman who had a child was on public assistance. Or why when these mothers cashed their checks, the *mujahids'* wives always escorted them, the cash funneling from the Ums' hands to the *mujahids'* wives' hands to the hands of Imam Isa's wives. Now she wanted a way out.

Living there for almost two years, Ummi was having cabin fever and wanted to see more than the insides of rooms. She'd met all of Imam Isa's wives, including the head wife, and was learning the games she had to play to get outside. My mother told the head wife she had a Macy's card. The wives wanted to use it to purchase for the Community, and to do that she had to go with them.

A plan came to her and she puffed herself up, preparing a speech as she walked across the street to the Wives' House. She told herself, *You're going with the wives and you're going to buy this, that, or the other with your card.* She waited outside the gates for the head wife and prayed the wife wouldn't see through her. But Ummi was right—as long as she had Macy's, she was able to buy a sliver of independence, which at the time was what she needed—a trip to a department store and back. This journey afforded her the opportunity to soak up sensations she didn't know she missed. Sensations that spoke up in whispered conversations from people who walked by or the sounds of canary-yellow checkered taxis as they blew horns at slow-moving pedestrians. Even the taxis' screeching stops in front of neon traffic lights made her giddy. She could smell the exhaust fumes from buses and aromas from hot dog stands while feeling the kinetic hurry of people, pigeons, and peddlers moving around her. Being free to leave the Community meant remembering what one's senses were meant for. It meant not hiding.

The card made Ummi feel something new—the Community had her, but she had the plastic. She was bargaining with a credit card for her right to walk beyond the Community, and it felt strangely powerful; it made her feel important, even better than some of the other Sisters. She always kept it in the back of her head to make sure that when she left the Community, they would have fully paid the bill. It hadn't occurred to her before how sheltered she had been, as though she were on a nineteenth-century plantation and forbidden from skipping beyond the confines of her master's land without a pass from the Big House. While she may not have seen that connection before brandishing the borrowed money, the card taught her the Community valued those who could survive.

Yet having the card also meant returning to the Community and remembering why they'd dropped out of the world in the first place. The hard faces of strangers and the allure of materialism. Fighting for one's piece on a pavement where people bumped into each other without apologies or acknowledgment of doing so. The stench emanating from the big stinking apple that rotted from the inside out. Ummi reveled in the choke of the city and was simultaneously turned off. Watching the bustle tired her out. Those crazy *kafirs* were confirmation she was good where she was.

Plus, the way people looked at them was never humane but rather a look of shock and wonderment, a look akin to seeing an exotic zoo animal. Adults outright stared, stopped in their tracks with gaping mouths. Ummi caught these looks in her periphery but wasn't perturbed. She had a crew who moved over those grimy streets as if they were cemented just for their feet. The more people stared, the higher their heads rose, the lighter they stepped, and the more they exuded their self-taught superiority over everyone they passed. Instead of making them feel like outcasts, the stares made them move like prophets among sinners who couldn't help wanting to look at examples so divine it rendered some of them speechless. Those Ums had no control over the awe they provoked and couldn't help people's reactions to it.

For Ummi, fighting with those fools every day was fruitless when all she wanted was a taste of normalcy every now and again, which the Macy's card offered. As important to Ummi was that it was a way for her to contribute beyond performing domestic duties. Ummi and the other Ums enjoyed floating through aisles of children's clothes as their hands grazed over cottons and wools, ruffles and buttons for children not their own. Ummi beamed at her ability to buy for the little ones, even if it was just for some of the children. As a woman who grew up with a grandmother who gave the bare minimum, Ummi couldn't help but see herself in every needy child. She happily put her plastic down and signed her name for new undershirts, socks, and wool tights that would later be worn by the children who needed them the most.

But the plan backfired. In addition to pink undies, cable-knit tights, children's leg warmers, and baby bed linens, Imam Isa's wives also began reaching for pantyhose, lacy lingerie, and silk scarves. Deep down, Ummi knew the scales of this compromise would eventually tip, her freedom and generosity in exchange for her self-respect. She asked herself how much she was willing to give for a few hours of play in a department store. Was she prepared to sacrifice her pride to be away from the Community? She thought about this and bit her tongue so as not to forfeit her newly acquired freedom. She sucked it up and struggled against the gravity of shame to keep her head raised. Ummi told herself it was a simple compromise. Anyone else in her position would do the same. Except the nauseating feeling of being duped didn't dissipate.

She was outside yet completely hidden from the world with a band of women who symbolized her but wielded more power. The power of those women being married to Imam Isa meant Ummi quietly agreed to buy for them when she didn't buy toothpaste, lotion, or toilet tissue for herself. Her initial feeling of contributing gave way to feeling like she was whoring herself out. Ummi's biggest question became one of mental survival. How was she going to protect her child if she was too afraid to stand up for herself? This process of awakening was like a person in a coma opening an eye for the first time to the searing sunlight splintering in through a hospital room window. It couldn't have hurt more if someone had said her mother had been alive all along and just didn't want her, so she disappeared. Admitting that things were bad was harder than making the decision to submit herself to the Community.

For months now, it had become clear to Ummi how she had become this woman—she had followed her husband. But to realize on her own she had to leave, with no encouraging words massaging her decision or having ultimatums thrown at her, meant she needed some kind of power or incident to propel her. Standing up for herself was something she never had in abundance or on reserve. If she had it, she would have come, seen, and left as quickly as Um Kalila had. Unfortunately, she was paralyzed with the foresight that if she left, my father would not follow.

Ummi knew she could limp along on a broken crutch for so long until she had to stand on her own. She asked herself which was worse—seeing the Community for what it was or pretending? Could she get the image of the Community's crooked playing field out of her head? She thought of how Imam Isa said everyone had to pull their weight, yet whenever she walked up to the gates of his house, she noticed not one of his wives had dark circles or bags under her eyes like she had. While she acquired a habit of twisting the material of her dress, as I did when I was nervous, his wives were calm and spoke as if humming. Many of the Sisters complained of hunger, yet when she saw Imam Isa's thick wives with curves that even yards of material couldn't hide, she refused to believe anyone in his home had an empty stomach.

The way they walked through the streets during the shopping excursions, as if they were not forgotten avenues walked long ago, proved the wives didn't spend all their days behind gates. It was one thing for everyone to sacrifice, but she could no longer ignore how one thing was preached and another practiced. To herself, she started questioning the ways of the Community, including the Houdini tricks they pulled when city officials stopped by. Like pulling a hippopotamus out of a hat or making a woman vanish, they did the seemingly impossible by making a plethora of adults and children, mats and mattresses, disappear before suspicious and annoyed women with clipboards and paperwork in totes rang their doorbells. Welfare did face-to-face visits inside homes, and Sisters who lived in the Community for a long time had its various addresses as theirs.

One day, with scarves tied around their heads and their dresses hiked up to their thighs, as if they were about to wade in water, the Ums carried cribs and cots, clothing and cubbies from the most visible rooms in one house to the basements and into closets of others. Infants, toddlers, little girls, boys, and women were ushered away and crammed into another house as if they were all away at camp. When everyone was gone, the Ums then scrubbed the kitchen and living room with rags drenched in Lysol and black soap. With sweaty brows and dirty fingernails, these women became synchronized moving companies who erased all evidence of too many people living in one house and replaced the empty spaces with the furniture, pictures, and personality of a single-family home. For two days the set stood until the weary welfare agent said she was satisfied and was back in her car, miles away until the next visit. Ummi wondered what was happening behind the scenes that so many people probably shared the same addresses and no one questioned it, unless many just dropped off the map altogether?

The first time Ummi participated in the disappearing act, she was floored by the organization it took to sway even the most suspicious. If she ignored certain uneasy truths before, she couldn't ignore the production of false living situations they created and got away with. She felt the Community had enough men, women, and children living in poor conditions to have the place shut down, but it remained standing. Ummi felt in her gut someone from Face-to-Face was being paid off, because they always had time to transform any house from a hellhole into a home before they got the knock on the door. The more she realized how they lied about our living arrangements, the more fearful she became of possibly losing me.

It seemed seeing me on a schedule, regardless of whether it was her schedule or not, was enough to sustain her. Never having an idle minute may have been part of the master plan to keep folks from questioning. Between twice-daily visitations, working and cleaning around the clock, and Islamic lessons, Ummi didn't have time to kick her heels up or even acknowledge her own breath.

Looking around at the number of men, women, and children who made up the Community, she realized we weren't crammed together because we were building a bond; we were overcrowded because someone was greedy. Ummi imagined the Department of Health doing an inspection and everyone going to jail and losing their children. When she saw my father, she tried to put him in her head.

"You know they would take Jamiyla and throw us into jail," she told him.

My father wasn't sensitive to drama, so he shooed these doubts the same way he did gnats. He seemed to live in denial, but Ummi's feelings couldn't be waved away any longer. The reality of what she had become in two years was recognizable to her. It wasn't just that she was practicing a new religion, that her child and husband seemed like distant memories of a love that once belonged to her, or that she could no longer remember what she used to smell like; she became the one thing she swore to never be and that was dependent. Money was important because it meant not having to ask for help, which opened up the possibility of rejection. But in the Community, Ummi, like so many other women, was on welfare. She would think of my father's speech about not slaving any longer and wondered what was welfare if not a slave system? She wasn't knocking Sisters who needed public assistance, but she didn't consider herself in need.

Considering Imam Isa's teachings and the strict life he forced on everyone, Ummi still didn't know what being Muslim meant to her. Did it mean sleeping swaddled in her clothes, sometimes with shoes on, mummified in multiple layers of blankets, or was it the joy she felt on *jumah*? There were times when the women had to take cold showers in an already freezing house, which made working at the Children's House that much more enviable because it always had heat and hot water.

Heightening the suffering were persistent rumors, increasing whispers about child abuse. Ummi started checking me from head to heel when she visited. Although she admitted to me decades later during one of our interviews that she was aware children were beaten on their hands and feet with rulers, she said I never appeared mistreated. There were never bruises. To her, my silence could have meant I didn't like the rules, or I was trying to make a statement by making no statement.

Growing up with a grandmother who used wire hangers and threw iron pots and pans at her with the force of bricks dropping into a calm pond, Ummi didn't see beating a child as a crime; the crime was lying to authorities for welfare checks and living with children in a house that was a potential fire hazard. She was growing tired of faking ignorance. The time had come for her to face her fear. Ummi would pull out her Macy's card and look at it, wishing she could buy courage with it the way she had bought herself a few hours of freedom.

Thirteen

The Betrayal

Ummi looked up the word "betrayal" and stared at the definition, which included the words "unfaithful" and "to disappoint." She sighed. Her desire to leave came in waves but fell like dominoes. It began with Um Kalila's abrupt exit and escalated to another dramatic attempt at an exit. Ummi started rebelling at work. She thought some Sisters resented the bond she had with another Sister, Um Sabina, who worked with her in Infants, and it angered her. She and Um Sabina worked as a hive. Unlike other rooms in the ward that had diapers and dirty bottles in cribs and on the floor, they kept their rooms spotless. This Sister didn't share prayers and secrets, but the affection she and Ummi had for one another rested in the babies they each adored as much as their own. Their adoration for the babies, however, was met with scorn and bad faith, because, as Ummi explained, the two of them were not solemn enough about their jobs. Ummi resisted her misery marauders, knowing they sucked their teeth and rolled their eyes because she worked with babies, the prized positions. The other reason Ummi resisted was that she and Um Sabina were working comrades. For some Sisters, these two reasons combined tasted too much like privilege, and the women were separated.

Before the split, Ummi worked during the day and balanced her time between the babies and me at night for *tifl* time. This was an ideal schedule until she was put on nights. Tired from working through the evening, Ummi slept during the day, which made it hard for her to see me, and she accepted the kindness of her friend Ni'mah, who offered to visit me when Ummi couldn't. Probably to appease Ummi, who was growing irritated with her schedule, she was named night supervisor. But she didn't want it. She didn't know how to be authoritative and, coupled with her impatience for the time it would have taken to train a person to reach her idea of perfection, she ultimately did most of the duties herself.

She soon grew tired of working double time and asked to return to the day shift. Even though there was an open position for the Salat Girls, she couldn't have the job because it was against the rules; I had aged up to that group when I turned four. Instead, she was placed with toddlers who wore cloth diapers that had to be dunked out and washed by hand. Baby crap was one thing, but a two-year-old's poopy pants was almost the same as an elderly person's to Ummi. Her stomach turned every time she had to change a child. Fed up with the toddlers, she asked again to be with the infants before being told no. Maybe the Community was now fed up with her as well.

Once when Ummi was serious about leaving, she was confronted by Um Sabina. On that day, they brawled and tussled until Ummi was too tired to lift herself off the floor, let alone walk out the door. She had no idea that just as Um Kalila had affected her, she had affected Um Sabina. Ummi didn't think anyone would try to stop her from leaving, believing no one cared enough, but these women did not back down from their beliefs. As with Um Kalila, the door had cracked open for Ummi, and she started to pray for her exit.

By some stroke of luck, Ummi was allowed to work with my group. This was better than freedom for her. Months had gone by where she had watched, snuck, and crept around just to catch glimpses of me, and now finally we were physically in the same room together every day. Ummi was so happy she could watch me with her two eyes from dawn to dusk she didn't know what to do with herself. She had forgotten how much she needed me near. But this lasted only a week before Sisters started talking. Then she was told she couldn't stay there and was sent back to the toddlers.

Seeing this as a sign of disrespect, she went on strike and refused to work. The standoff might have been brief, but the Ums saw her differently. No longer so demure. Or maybe they thought she was a dormant firecracker waiting for the spark of a match to set her off. They couldn't have been sure which it was, but they had to know she was changing.

Around this time, when Ummi slept during the day, exhausted from her night shifts, Um Ni'mah would take me outside to play with her sons in the yard. Ummi liked her gestures because she didn't want me to feel abandoned. She didn't want me to forget what it was like to be a child. By Um Ni'mah showing an interest, Ummi knew someone was keeping an eye on me when hers were closed or when she was too tired to get dressed.

Then things started to get strange. My father never said it, but Ummi learned he was being penalized. Instead of peddling like the rest of the Brothers, my father was inside performing menial maintenance jobs. Whenever she asked him for information on anything, he never gave a straight answer. When she asked why he was inside, he would only say he had gotten into trouble. Maybe he had mentioned something about his quota to her; she wasn't sure. All she knew was that he was on probation and stuck inside like her, and that was nothing to ignore. But she let his issue go. That is, until a Sister pulled the veil from Ummi's eyes.

"Don't you know your mate and Ni'mah were caught in a closet together?" the Sister said to Ummi.

Ummi thought, Who was this man who seduced her into loving him, marrying him, giving him a child, and then moving into the Community? Who was this man who could then seduce another woman in a closet? It was a blow, like a hit over the head with a lead pipe. She had trusted that woman with her child when all the while the woman was sneaking around with her husband. It seemed everyone in the Community knew except for Ummi. While she slept, the two people she trusted the most were deceiving her. And to make it worse, they got caught in the closet like little kids with their pants down. She imagined she was so tired from protesting that she was blinded by it.

When she eventually saw Um Ni'mah, she told her to stay away from me. Ummi wanted so badly to kick Um Ni'mah's teeth out, claw her eyes, and rip her *khimar* off her face and choke her with it. She had never felt so violent in her life. As Um Ni'mah denied the affair, Ummi kept thinking how she was trying to steal her family from her. It felt like something out of a movie. Then she confronted my father, who said nothing happened and that folks were blowing into a deflated balloon. Ummi asked where his self-respect was. His reply was if he wanted to take another wife, he could and he wouldn't have to talk to her about it.

Ummi believed her husband thought she was the same doe-eyed girl he had brought into the Community two years before. But she wasn't. She was taught a husband had to consult his first wife before taking another, and all wives and children were to be looked after. The fact that he wasn't taking care of me meant he did not have deeper pockets to take care of others. She was stunned by how he tried to justify being caught with another woman. Thinking of what to do, she grappled at the little bit of pride she had left, and the first chance she got she called the big house and told the head wife what happened. Ummi told her she wanted Um Ni'mah to stay as far away from her family as California was from New York. She wanted the wife's empathy. She had to have known what Ummi was feeling, being a first wife, and Ummi felt she owed her for all the secret Macy's outings they had taken together. Plus, she had never asked her for anything before. She must have granted Ummi's wish, because Um Ni'mah stayed clear of her path and mine.

Who would have thought this simple act of standing up for herself would have brought silence from other Sisters? They didn't like how she was able to make one phone call and get what she wanted. But what did they know? Nothing. Ummi felt none of them seemed to care that her daughter's well-being was at stake. How any mother could let some woman who was trying to ruin her marriage run around the Community with her child was a mystery to her. Those same Sisters didn't even want her around their babies even though that was her job. How could they not feel?

By this point Ummi was so full of rage anything could have set her off. She asked one more time to go back to Infants and when she was told no, she went on strike again. She sat in the Sisters' Quarters, crossed her arms, and said, "I'm not leaving this house. You do whatever you have to, but I'm going nowhere." Everyone was silenced by her unwillingness to do as she was told, because she was always so eager to please before. Ummi thought of herself as a servant of God, what the Community called a true *amatullah*, only to discover she was a servant to the Community. She had been hit in too many of the same sore spots and was a walking wound by this point. She told the Sister in charge she could either put her back with the Salat Girls or put her with the infants, but she was not going back to toddlers.

This went on for days: Ummi refusing to work, Imam Isa's wives telling her she had to. Ummi wanted to do what she wanted to do. She felt these people owed her for mishandling her mind and her marriage. She was done with their rules and invisible whips and calmly gathered the hem of her dress along with her courage and made that dreadful phone call to Grandma. Grandma was the last person Ummi wanted to ask for help because it was her son whom she was trying to get away from, but she thought she had no one else to turn to.

When Ummi came to get me, carrying a small bag on her shoulder and another in her hand, we walked down the stairs and she opened the front door. We were both amazed to be on the other side, watching the door close us out as we waited in the cold, bright winter day for Grandma to drive up in her blue Chevy. When Grandma arrived, she popped the trunk for our two small bags, waited for Ummi to secure me in the back seat and close her door, and then she drove off. Grandma asked about my father, and Ummi told her he was out peddling. We didn't wait for his return because he would have tried to talk her out of leaving, and Ummi felt she might have listened.

It happened anyway. My father immediately worked at her weak spots, telling her our family was all she had. He even had two of Imam Isa's wives call Grandma's house, promising things would be different. So we went back a week later to start all over again.

I don't remember those days at Grandma's, but I can't forget returning to those same gates and that same door, ringing the same bell we'd rung two years before. Before I knew it, I was back on the blue mat looking for a spot to rest my head where a little girl's foot wouldn't be. Apparently unaware I had left, the girls weren't surprised to see me. The Ums didn't seem to care. My return garnered no fanfare or commentary. We girls moved through our time in the Community like links in a chain, weaving individual fear, restlessness, and sadness into each other when we slept, with legs intertwined and feet stacked. We seemed to only recognize another or ourselves as individuals when one of the links was strained, rubbed another the wrong way, or broke. Our differences were acknowledged only after one of us reminded others of her need to be seen as an individual. It was only when one broke the collective repetition that we all stopped, looked around, and admitted sadness lived within the rooms and between cracks in the walls and floors.

My departure wasn't enough to shift anyone's interest, because my emotional outbursts were surely seen as unnecessary dramas. The Ums may have been secretly happy I left, and the Salat Girls probably didn't notice. For all I knew, someone else could've arrived in that week to fill the vacant spot in the room, and she could have been a better version of the one I left behind. Obedient. Or a master of indifference.

Neither of which I was. When I returned, the girls and Ums created space but did not welcome me back. The girls may have wanted to ask how it felt to be with my family, to speak English without caution, to eat when I wanted, and to spend more than an hour a day with my mother, but they didn't. There was nowhere to speak in private. Angry, I cried a broken heart, half-crazy I had escaped but was somehow back in the same cell.

As for Ummi, leaving her floor-bed meant she had nothing to sleep on. One of the Sisters offered her bed to share because she worked during the day while Ummi worked at night. They rotated like this for seven days, with Ummi being reminded of sharing a bed with her grandmother, her cousins, and her friend Yvette from school. She thought of her life as a child and her life now as an adult and disliked the parallels. Her husband was a fool. She was afraid. I was depressed. Plus, Ummi needed to regain control. A week away from the cold draft of the Community was enough to shock her into loving the blasting heat of a radiator and the softness of a queen-size bed. She couldn't forget having a door that locked, sleeping with her child next to her, taking hot showers, and eating rice and beans and apple pie. If seven days had been enough for God to create the universe, then seven days was enough for her to realize this chapter of her life was over.

Just as it happened the week before, when Ummi had come to my door, heavy heels hitting the floor and her brassy voice filling the room, she came again with two small bags, scooped me in her arms, and said goodbye to everyone she saw. Grandma pulled up to the same curb in front of the white house, popped the trunk, waited for Ummi to strap me in the back seat and close her passenger door, and drove off. We were back in Harlem at my grandmother's house just as we had been the week before, although this time, we never looked back. A few weeks later, we were in Brooklyn at Mrs. Hargis's.

PART TWO

Acclimate

Fourteen

Ninie's World (1981)

We left the Community months ago, and it was Mrs. Hargis, whom I affectionately called Ninie, with whom we moved in. I saw her simply as a grandmother but felt she and Ummi had a history unbeknownst to me—of a shitty grandfather, a cheating father, an escape from a cult—a history I wanted no part of. At Ninie's, outside the Community, I felt I'd stumbled into a multidimensional life that was like wearing 3D movie glasses. The world was cinematic even though Ninie shunned sunlight by keeping her first-floor window blinds half closed and the dark, heavy curtains drawn. The large apartment's dark furniture and carpeted floors also absorbed light, but I didn't care. I was free, and Ninie provided yards of rein. A short, thick woman with a busty bosom and a hobbled walk, Ninie also called me Ninie. We spoke the same language, and the double talk drove Ummi mad.

"Don't you two ever get confused when you call each other the same thing?" she asked. "Jamiyla will say Ninie and you'll reply, 'Yes, Ninie.' How do you not get confused?"

"Because we know who we are" was Ninie's response.

Ninie liked to dye her short white hair the blackest black and would draw in her missing eyebrows with a brown pencil to warm up her light complexion. If anyone was ever confused by her lack of brows and facial expression, Ninie would clarify with cusswords that rolled off her tongue and out of her mouth with the same ease as the smoke from her Chesterfield cigarettes. She became extra spunky when sipping her favorite drink, whiskey on ice with 7UP, and because there was very little entertainment in the apartment except for whatever came on Channel 7, Ninie teased us.

"Why you still dress like that, all covered up?" Ninie would ask Ummi. "No one from that place is watching." I would listen, searching for a reasonable answer from Ummi, but she would simply bristle, stiffen her posture, and pull her hijab tighter around her head to show how little she tolerated religious disrespect. Hardly anything seemed funny to Ummi.

Outside on the street, textures and colors were more alive, more vivid than they had been inside the Community. The bustling of bodies was like choreography. The air hung heavy with cigarette smoke and car exhaust fumes. Snagging my attention were the strangers, who wore reds, blues, whites, and purples all at once, an explosion of colors that stood in stark contrast to the monochromatic greens and browns I was used to. Women wore feathered hair that settled atop their heads and around their faces like a bird's nest, and little Black and Puerto Rican girls wore rainbow-colored beads or barrettes in their hair. The trees seemed to tower higher over my head with lush leaves that hummed whenever they rustled. My senses were turned up and I inhaled everything—from the slight hint of sewer stench that wafted up from belowground, forcing me to temper my breathing and inhale in quick intervals, to the cracked concrete below my feet that graciously offered little yellow daisies to passersby.

I loved being outside even as I felt stifled by Ummi's superstitions and prejudices, which she ramped up when we were in public. "Don't make eye contact with white people or let them touch you," she told me. "Same for dogs. If one licks you, you'll have to take seven baths." The Community didn't have mirrors—Isa said they were a sign of vanity—so we avoided them. I didn't ask for McDonald's when we passed one or when I saw a child exit one, hungrily sifting through the paper bag to get to the Happy Meal kids' toy inside, because I thought hamburgers were sinful for containing the word "ham." Ummi and I didn't go outdoors often, but when we did, people either stared at us or would make room by circumventing away from our strange orbit.

Like the formerly imprisoned, who are happy to be released from captivity but unaware and afraid of how the world has changed, we interacted cautiously and rarely with people who hadn't experienced the Community. Ummi said they were all *kafirs*, non-Muslims, and not as connected to God as we were. When I asked her if that meant my grandmother and Ninie were *kafirs* also, she said yes. "They might be our family, but they are different from us," Ummi told me. She was teaching me the lessons she had learned from the Community. As we had done in the Community, we didn't discuss our feelings but continued as we had done over the two years when we were inside—unrolling our prayer rugs to make *salat* five times a day and adding Arabic to our speech the way people peppered meals to fill in what was missing.

A strange paradox emerged that while some aspects of the Community loomed large over Ummi and me, other pieces began to morph and disappear. One day, the Community was all I thought about, a house I felt acutely aware of as something threatening that I had escaped with luck. Another day, the Community felt like a bad dream, a past life that had occurred in a different universe. I was beginning to forget why we had rituals that no one else I knew had.

Subconsciously, I started peeling off the layers of the Community like a film reel spooled in reverse. If Ninie wasn't engrossed in soap operas or the news, I was running through the dial of our wooden console radio in search of Rick James, Blondie, Prince. Ninie told me she didn't like quiet kids, but using my voice was a throat-clearing exercise filled with hesitations, whispers, and fears. What if I said the wrong thing and Ummi sent me back to the Ums, who never hesitated to correct me? Ninie promised she would never again let that happen, which opened the gates for me to gab incessantly.

Six months had flown by since we'd left the Community, with Ummi continuing to say very little but quietly changing in other ways. She took down her veil, neatly folded it up, and shut it away in an unused dresser drawer. She would bring reddish-brown henna powder home from the local Muslim shop that she would mix with warm water and shellac and apply on her face as a mask. Rings appeared on her fingers like bejeweled knuckles. Slowly, she was unshrouding, baby-stepping away from anonymity. Her veil was gone, but Ummi still had no interest in conforming to another's expectations, unless it was specific to being a Muslim mother, an energy and identity she seemed to vibrate through her pores.

Ninie countered Ummi's vibrations with a juvenile response that grated Ummi's nerves. If Ummi declared that it was time for *salat*, Ninie would say there was no harm in letting me finish watching *The Facts of Life* or *The Jeffersons*. When Ummi tried to cook halal, in separate pots and pans from what she cooked Ninie's food in, Ninie would brush a piece of pork across my lips, secretly offer me a sip of her whiskey, and slip me a piece of the broccoli that was cooked with lard.

"Ain't it hypocritical for you to even be around this stuff?" Ninie asked. She knew Ummi had no other choice so long as we lived there.

When Ummi and I studied the alphabet or she read a book to me, she would pause and remind me that people might tease me when I started school. I had no reference for that word until she whispered "Ninie," who had spent half the year trying to get under Ummi's skin and now started to mock me whenever I made *salat*. During Ramadan that year, Ninie tormented me by offering to sneak bits of food and water my way when Ummi wasn't looking. She laughed when I slipped on my green dresses and brown shoes, saying I looked like a child from another era.

"I grew up in Jim Crow South with two sisters that I despised, but I still never looked as pitiful as you do," Ninie told me.

I had forgotten so much Arabic during those first few months with Ninie that the three prayers I said every night before going to bed and the prayer I said before eating meals were the only pieces that stuck.

Ninie joked that I had gone to jail to come out as the same person I was when I went in. "Don't you think it funny that she went to school to learn Arabic, but it's you who has to remind her to mind her language?" Ninie asked Ummi. Ummi would respond with raised eyebrows, but no more. She was showing me how to rise above, how to remain poised.

Ninie knew which volcanic buttons to press on Ummi and would sit back bemused after Ummi simmered with so much intensity because of the teasing that she would stop speaking to us both for an entire day. Ummi's verbal protests illustrated to me that she was hell-bent on being steadfast. She also made her commitment clear by weaving Arabic through her meanings when speaking to me. The veil was gone, but her nose ring and hijab remained intact. She told me that while other children said "Mom," she would always be Ummi to me.

As an adult, Ummi told me she continued to believe in and practice Islam, even though she remained unsure if what we had practiced in the Community could be called Islam. "I had some serious doubts about the Community's teachings once we were gone, but I held on to the discipline and to the other pieces of Islam that were most beautiful to me, like the language and devotion to God," Ummi had told me. She confirmed that about a month after she and I left the Community for good, my father walked out also.

"Then why weren't we three together?" I asked her. "Why were we still separated?"

We had been on the telephone having a random conversation about the courses I was taking for my senior year in college and being too broke to pay for cable when I pivoted and randomly asked if she thought the Community killed their relationship or had it been dead on arrival. The entire situation was confusing to me: my father claiming he wanted to become Muslim to move into a community that separated him from his family, which is the opposite of what a Muslim family should look like, to the three of us leaving separately, on separate occasions, and not coming together.

"It was complicated, but I wouldn't leave Ninie's," Ummi said. "I knew he couldn't take care of us like he was supposed to, and Ninie made it easy for us to stay with her because she made sure we really didn't need or want for anything, which your father did not like and to which I did not care."

I thought back to my father's absence during that time and how little it mattered then. We had left the Community first, but its effects lingered. Ummi didn't need anyone to push Community guilt on her; she pushed it on us both. When I investigated her face those first few months after we'd left, the outline of her bitterness appeared like a sketch in progress. Strange to me was that the resentment didn't make her defiant; it made her want to be better than my father. There were days when I could feel her pride rise above her like a crown. Becoming Muslim might have been my father's idea, but it was Ummi who had soaked up the training for how to soldier through. She believed in the Community's self-taught self-righteousness. I sensed she had found something, a purpose, from the Community. Looking and doing differently didn't seem to faze her, but it bothered me.

One evening before bed, I whined that I wanted to say my prayers in English, get on my knees in front of the bed, and put my palms together like I'd seen people do on television. Ummi responded by plucking my lips, her long nails catching the bottom one. She gripped my chin and said, "You're Muslim, which means you're not like everyone else, which means you say your prayers in Arabic." I was afraid to tell her my Arabic felt like dissipating smoke, that it was becoming harder to grasp with each passing day. Her Arabic skills seemed to expand to the point of taking up space. As distant as the Community felt to me—past life, dreamlike—it remained in the recesses of my brain because of the swath it occupied in Ummi's life, from the hijab she still wore to the "*coo fattah*" she would say, her invented cue for me to pray after I'd brushed my teeth and put on Winnie-the-Pooh pajamas.

I didn't know why, but my prayer station was always in front of the bed. I stood facing the open door to the living room, as if in performance.

Ninie always watched from the guest of honor seat, on the huge green sofa's middle cushion, which was encased in plastic. From her perch, which offered an unobstructed view of me, she would mimic my movements as cigarette smoke wafted up and around her black hair. Ummi didn't find Ninie's antics funny, but she also wouldn't close the door. Unable to chide Ninie, Ummi growled low at me to stop being silly.

"You still answer to me," Ummi said quietly. "Ninie won't save you forever."

"I'm just trying to prep the girl for what she's going to encounter outside," Ninie yelled from the living room. "Don't be so hard on her."

Ninie made fun of me, but she also spoke up for me. In the Community, I had never heard adults argue for children being children the way they argued for and forced us into hushed clones of each other. Ninie encouraged my personality, egged me on as I performed Michael Jackson moves around the house, and ignored my interruptions of her nightly news at six. I loved Ninie, and I also knew she tested Ummi's patience with jokes about crazy Muslims.

While Ninie constantly probed Ummi about wearing a rag on her head, as she called it, Ummi was most perturbed when Ninie mocked my prayers. If I messed up the recital and started giggling, Ummi would tower over me and say, "God is nothing to laugh at."

I would grumble, "But Ninie is making fun of me."

Ummi would respond, "I know, and I don't care. You can't be so easily distracted by teasing."

I would pull it together but wonder if Ummi was taking her frustrations out on me, similar to when I'd learned my Ums had children and decided they treated my group callously because they were bitter about their own separations. Like the Ums, Ummi's look would ask, Why aren't you taking this seriously? Don't you realize all I have sacrificed? Ummi said as much to me one night after my prayers as we stood in our usual spots in the bedroom. With our rolled-up prayer rugs leaned up against a corner in the walk-in closet, she told me to sit on the bed.

"You may have forgotten, but I have sacrificed much for this belief system," she said. "I abandoned my own identity, took lessons from others who might have been just as lost as I was, turned my back on family members who refused to visit because they said I acted holier than thou. I know you're a child, but I'm not going to allow anyone to make fun of my religion."

She then turned to Ninie, who was sitting in her usual spot on the sofa, and politely asked her to stop making fun of my prayers.

"If you love this child like you say and don't want her in trouble, please stop teasing her," Ummi said.

Like a kid caught with a mouthful of candy, Ninie became defensive. The top half of her body pitched forward like she was going to stand up. "I'm not doing anything to that child," she said from the living room. "I'm sitting way out here and she's in there with you, where you're always standing over her like some prison guard. How could I be bothering her? I'm just looking."

I didn't understand why Ummi was so upset, especially as I no longer saw the pretty rug she used to kneel on, bending headfirst, or saw her make *wudhu* before quietly reciting the sacred words under her breath as if they were secrets. I remembered seeing her do this daily at Ninie's when we'd first arrived, but I also noticed she had stopped. I resented this double standard. When I asked Ummi why she didn't use her prayer rug anymore, she told me to do as she said.

Every night, I put my left hand over my right and placed both in the middle of my chest. Remembering the movements from watching me perform them, Ninie started to synchronize the steps, sometimes doing them before I did. While I said my prayers in Arabic, I would also wonder why Ummi no longer did the same before she went to sleep. Why was I the only one forced to go to bed with the Community on my mind? Ummi had replaced my Ums from the Community, making it so I lost four and got one for life. Ninie, on the other hand, represented something new, something that felt like the opposite of discipline and order and oddly like preparation.

Fifteen

Chaos in Kindergarten

On the first day of kindergarten, Ummi placed me between her legs on a pillow, sat behind me on the sofa, and braided my hair straight back in eight crooked cornrows. After, she pulled out the ironing board and neatly pressed any stubborn wrinkles out of my green dress. She placed my newly made hard brown shoes at the door for me to step into on the way out, which Ummi had handcrafted by a cobbler who constructed the shoes directly from foam imprints of my feet to fix their leftward lean. The shoes were almost the same color as my paper lunch bag, which was filled with a bologna-and-cheese sandwich, an apple, and a small glass apple juice bottle. Once I was dressed, with my hijab in place, Ummi helped shimmy my arms through my small backpack, which housed a black-and-white composition book, a pink plastic pencil case with two new yellow #2 pencils and a white plastic ruler, and a box of rainbow-colored crayons.

"You're a big girl now," Ninie said.

I was circling the living room in my socks, steeling myself to be around another adult I didn't know, to share a small room with small, strange children. Ummi gripped my hand and pulled me closer toward the door. She tugged at my hijab, pulled it lower on my forehead. She motioned for me to put my shoes on, nodded that I knew what to do when I looked up at her with my fingers holding the laces.

"We've practiced this" was her answer to my silent question. "You know how to do this."

When she opened the door, my stomach fluttered like a dying butterfly. I wondered if Ummi would see my metamorphosis. My lips shined with Vaseline, and I smelled of Dove soap and cocoa butter, religiously applied by Ummi to my left arm to heal a forgotten burn scar. I hesitated at the apartment's threshold, but Ummi and her stomach ushered me down the building's corridor, past the doorman, and through the back door, which opened to the playground and the elementary school. Wasting no time, Ummi told me how to behave.

"Do not talk in school. I want you to learn and then come back home," she said. "I'm not going to pick you up because you're right here. Be my star."

I was smiling. I wanted Ummi to know all I wanted was for her to acknowledge I was good. To be somewhere where I could speak. I had somehow wiped handfuls of the Community from my memory, but I remembered the sadness and loneliness and hoped this school would be different. Ummi dropped her big belly to my height and pulled me into it. She gave me a kiss and hug, yanked my hijab farther down my forehead, and made me promise one thing.

"Promise you will not salute the flag," she said. "If the teacher asks why, you say it's against your religion." I didn't understand what religion had to do with a flag, but before I could ask about it, Ummi stood up and spun me around in one motion. "Have a good first day. I love you," she said.

I knew she watched as I walked away, but I didn't look back. My heavy shoes clunked, and it took all my concentration to not kick myself in the ankles. When I reached the kindergarteners' line, some kids looked at me with narrowed or widened eyes. The boys wore Wrangler jeans, sneakers, and light sweaters and the girls had on knee-length, pleated skirts, white button-down shirts, and black or white patent-leather Mary Jane shoes. I wore a long green dress Ummi had hand-sewed and brown-laced shoes that felt like wooden planks. Even the teachers, who were weaving in and out of children to help them line up by different grades, stared at me. Ummi had said for months after the Community that we were different, and now, looking at the other kids, I didn't like it.

I wasn't as resolute in my role as a Muslim girl as Ummi was in her role as a Muslim mother and wife, and I was fine with my position. I told myself I would do everything I could to stop being Muslim, to stop being forced to be someone I wasn't. I believed in a god but wasn't sure if that god was Allah or, as my father's mother believed, Jesus. I couldn't imagine a god who let bad things happen to children and left them to fend for themselves. I wasn't sure I believed Ummi's belief system, that women should cover up and pray separately from their husbands and walk five paces behind him, as she had been taught. I believed women were as powerful as men, girls as strong as boys.

A freckle-faced redheaded boy turned to me and shattered my thoughts. "Why are you dressed like that?" he demanded. "You don't have any clothes?"

I quickly realized he was talking to me and grew warm from my feet upward. Girls covered their mouths and laughed. Boys backed him up and murmured, "She's weird." I remained quiet; I heard Ummi say, *Be a good girl.* The teacher looked back at everyone, then at me. I refused to cry in front of kids I didn't know but felt like doing something. Like kicking Red Head in the knees with my big shoes. I recalled the story Ninie told me about her older sister smashing a brick into her left knee, almost breaking it. I imagined my heavy shoes doing the same to this boy.

The teacher told everyone to calm down. To Red Head, she asked, "And who made you the class clown? For that, you'll be the example of what happens when we're rude to our classmates. You're going to the corner."

I picked my head up and moved my feet forward. Red Head made snarling sounds at me as my class proceeded, but I pretended he didn't exist. After walking side by side with the boys, shortest to tallest, down a long hallway the color of dandelions and mayonnaise, we made it to our classroom, which was painted in baby blues and sunshine yellow. It was a large, airy room with blue floor mats and twenty chairs planted upside down on top of ten desks. Pasted to the walls were pictures of leaves crayoned in reds, oranges, yellows, and greens.

"Sit wherever you like," the teacher said. Her voice was warm, trusting, confident.

We all stood still at first, like small puppets waiting for someone to pull a string. I surveyed the room, wondered who was going to sit where. I didn't want to be the first to move, me in the hot-green dress and hot hair, noisy shoes, and knobby knees. I waited.

"Children," the teacher said, raising her voice slightly. "Please, pick a seat and sit down or I'll pick them for you."

The string twitched and our knees lifted. We feverishly zeroed in on the chair that would become ours for the rest of the year. I saw this round-faced girl with dimples and thick brown hair twisted with BoBo's grab a seat next to this boy with big blue eyes. I sat next to her. She looked nice, and I wanted her to be my friend. Her shirt was white, her skirt blue, her shoes were black patent leather, and she wore short white bobby socks with laced ruffle trimmings around the ankles. Her only jewelry was a small pair of gold star-shaped stud earrings. I wore three brass bracelets on my left wrist and tiny gold hoops in my ears. By the time I noticed Red Head was sitting directly across from me, every seat had been taken.

Mrs. Easton introduced herself as our kindergarten teacher. She said her job was to teach us to be good students, to play, rest, to master the alphabet, and then to read and write. But first, roll call. While Mrs. Easton read out Spanish, Chinese, and African American names, I thought how easy school was going to be in between everyone's "here."

I already knew my ABCs and how to play. I had been around kids longer than I'd been alone and knew how to share. I wasn't going to say anything unless Mrs. Easton asked me to speak.

It was when she said "Nicole Chisholm," and I didn't answer, that my confidence crumbled. I wondered how many times she called that name before I said, "Me." The kids were laughing. Not only was I the only one who said "me"—everyone else apparently said "here"—I obviously didn't know who I was either. From age two, Ummi exclusively called me Jamiyla, and Ninie called me Ninie. Ummi did teach me to write "Nicole" as my own name, but I didn't make the connection that people would also call me that name. I'd made my second embarrassing mistake and it was still the first day. As the laughs quieted and I lowered my head, Mrs. Easton continued with roll call.

The sun shifted over our singing of the ABC song, numbers, coloring, and story time. Mrs. Easton said it was lunchtime. I watched as everyone pulled their Scooby-Doo, Smurfs, or Barbie lunch boxes from under the desks. I was horrified. I didn't have a box and was too ashamed to show I had no Thunder Cats on my bag. I was hungry but hungered more to disappear. But then it was recess, and we were released into the large concrete-paved gated yard to run off lunch. With big leaps, I ran until my ankles felt like weights. I knew how to play alone. Over the flapping sound of the wind whipping through my hijab, I heard the muted sounds of a boy's squeaky voice.

"You're a freak," the voice squealed behind me. I stopped. I couldn't imagine why someone would bother the girl running in circles by herself. The voice belonged to the skinny, red-haired, freckle-faced boy from class.

"Stop running from me, you freak," he said. Then he was walking up to me, his red sneakers squeezing.

"Why are you dressed funny?" he demanded. I looked around at a small cluster of kids who started to gather, as if we were in a padded ring getting ready to wrestle.

"Why are your shoes so big?" Red Head asked. He laughed, and I swore it echoed around the yard.

"And why do you wear that thing on your head?" He pointed to my hijab. "What are you hiding?"

I mumbled nothing and slowly backed away.

"I want to know what's under that thing," he said. He reached for my head.

Reflex forced my neck to snap back and my feet to take flight. I bumped into the kids' circle, stumbled, then ran straight. I didn't look back but heard the squeaky voice and shoes behind me, calling me poor, weird, ugly. It didn't matter that I had private access to a swimming pool and lifeguards not many steps from my door. It didn't matter that my mother didn't have to work or that Ninie provided me with more love than I knew what to do with. None of that mattered except that I was wearing a homemade dress and handmade shoes and that I looked weird. Compared to everyone else, I stood out.

As I ran, I could feel him almost stepping on my heels. When I tried to pivot, he grabbed a handful of material and tore off my hijab. I spun around to see him smiling as if the green material were his prize. He jumped up and down pumping small fists into the air. To the few kids nearby he said, "Look at the freak's hair."

I stood in front of the entire yard, feeling naked with dozens of blue, brown, and green eyes on me, hopefully unaware of the tiny wet pearls rolling down my cheeks. I stood there, watching Red wave my hijab in front of my face as if I were a bull he was enticing to charge. Angry, I demanded my hijab back "before," and he cut me off.

"Before what?" he said.

I didn't know what to say or what I was going to do. Then Mrs. Easton was upon us, removing Red and me from the small crowd and the playground altogether, forcing us to sit with her inside the classroom. I curled up on a mat not far from Red, feeling cool air on my head. My hands went to my head in search of my hijab and realizing it was gone, I pulled at the bottom of my heavy cotton dress instead, tucking and folding so I had something to hold on to until class was over. This feeling of alienation from other children was a foreign concept. Kids didn't tease other kids in the Community because we were too disciplined to misbehave. And if we did misbehave, we knew the consequences. Plus, men, women, and children all dressed the same; how could anyone stand out? Kindergarten was not the Community.

When the rest of the class returned from recess, they joined Red and me on the mats for a nap until we were all awakened to go home. Outside, some parents were waiting to take their daughters and sons by the hand, discuss their first day of school as they walked home. I threw my backpack, with my composition book and pencils, over my two bony shoulders and walked around the schoolyard to the back entrance of my building.

I walked past the security guard and white walls, past the bronze fountain overflowing with wish pennies, and click-clacked down my building's hallway to our apartment, a survivor of a first day at school. Standing on tiptoe I rang the doorbell. Ummi and her belly opened the door, looking tall and weary. As I walked through the door, I could feel questions hanging in the air. Before saying hello or asking how my day was or what I had learned, Ummi asked what happened to my hijab.

"She got into some trouble," Ninie predicted, pitching forward on the green sofa. "Something happened and she got into trouble."

I didn't replay the battle, but I did say I didn't want a brown bag, green dress, or brown shoes ever again. With her long arms crossed in front of her, Ummi asked why not.

"Because none of the other kids are dressed like this," I yelled.

"That's because they're not Muslim. You are," she said, frowning. She pulled me into the apartment and closed the door. I wanted to say I was sick of being Muslim.

Instead, I said, practically screaming, "I want to be able to eat anything like the kids at school. None of them carry a paper bag. They have Scooby-Doo lunch boxes!"

I looked to Ninie for help, but she looked back with a cocked head and a frowned upper lip. Ummi didn't understand because she wasn't in my class. She didn't see how the teacher looked at me, like I was the kid she would have to protect for the rest of the year. Or how the girl with the BoBo's and bobby socks looked at me with pity.

"Jamiyla, kids are going to make fun of things they don't understand, and you can't change every time someone doesn't understand you," Ummi tried to rationalize. "You can't let teasing bother you."

I knew she wanted me to be bigger, bigger than everyone and everything, but I was a four-year-old who didn't want to go back to school dressed as some orphan wearing a hijab that would be ripped off my head again and I didn't want to be Muslim. Not being Muslim was my real argument.

To prove her "kids will be kids" theory was right, Ummi sent me to school the next day in the same uniform. Like the day before, Red chased me around the playground until he was able to grab a handful of my hijab, swiftly pulling it off with one hard tug.

"Give it back!" I screamed.

"Give it back or else what?" Red asked. With all the defiance stored in his little body, he asked, "Are you going to hit me?" And just like that, as if a director yelled "Action!" my right fist reached out and punched him on the nose. Blood instantly materialized, and he used the material he held in his hands to cover his face. Backing away, he screamed a muffled, "She hit me! She hit me!"

Mrs. Easton ran over, took one look at him, and pushed us both inside the classroom with her hands on our backs. While Mrs. Easton smothered my bully with ice bags and cold paper towels, I rattled on about the crowd, the chase, then the tug, which led to the bloody nose. I expected her to send me home, whip out a ruler and grab my feet, but she took my hand and said, "Okay. I understand. You two will stay here with me."

When I returned home after school and stood in the living room near the door with the bloody hijab in my left hand, my face streaked with dusty tear lines, Ninie stood up from the sofa with more energy than I'd ever seen. She pointed her bent, white finger in my direction but glared at Ummi.

"I told you she was having a hard time and now look. Blood," Ninie said. Her short black hair, now lined at the roots with pure white new growth, was shaking with the rest of her.

"How many times?" Ninie hissed. "I told you, I told you, I told you. Stop making her suffer for your mistakes."

"All right" was all Ummi said.

Sixteen

Sticks and Stones

After the kindergarten incident, Ummi's mantra was sticks and stones never killed anyone, but what did she know? Some wounds only needed a simple dressing, while others required sutures. She wasn't at school with me, running away from taunts in a long, stiff dress. Adults knew how to smile in their victim's face, wait until the person passed before secretly bad-mouthing them. Adults opted for silent stares instead of incivility. I had learned that kids were different.

Ummi's body was as rigid as a statue and her face perpetually set in stone whenever we left the apartment for whatever awaited us on cracked Brooklyn sidewalks or in brightly lit supermarket aisles. When we went out to buy milk or go to the bank, people quietly gawked, but Ummi seemed unperturbed. She said she didn't expect the curious to understand her. I, on the other hand, didn't like the looks. I hadn't had whatever training Ummi had received inside the Community to help shield me against ostracism, so I continued to live out some of its aspects: the hijab continued to be a fixture on our public heads, prayers stayed said in Arabic, and my father remained as emotionally and physically distant as he had been in the Community.

Yet Ummi continued to miss the Community, as far as I was concerned. The Community had provided her with a network of men and women who were the closest she ever had to having brothers and sisters. On the inside, they were an inseparable team. A woman who went outside always traveled with a cluster of other women. When people stopped and studied their covered faces, wondered if they were hot, disfigured, abused or not, they weren't alone. They stood out like purple people in space suits, but no one withstood ridicule or finger-pointing alone. In the Community, Ummi walked the streets with confidence, looking everyone in the eyes. She and her Sisters were a veil-wearing, Qur'an-reciting, no-pork-eating band of women who could have easily asked a *mujahid* to fix a situation and it would have been done. Defending themselves was a nonissue because no one in Bushwick bothered them. In the minds of many Community members, they were superior, more spiritual, and unquestionably more special than everyone else.

Once on the outside, alone, without a chorus, we didn't feel better than anyone else. On the outside, without those women, Ummi bowed her head. Moving through those streets without another adult with whom to speak her patchwork language, she was a young woman who wondered where she fit in. New York, even within the perimeters of our building's complex and neighborhood, was a bewildering puzzle. Ummi walked fast, blurred through checkout lines and across crosswalks like she was speeding away from something or didn't want anyone to look at her for long. Ummi missed her Sisters; their very existence reinforced her place as a cog in the Community's system. In the real world, there were no such reinforcements. Even our family chafed at our continued head coverings and Ummi's need to take it so far, when we were free to be whatever we wanted, as Ninie and my grandmother often said.

"How far are you going to take it?" Grandma asked Ummi during one of our visits to her.

"Aren't you tired of looking like that?" Ninie pushed constantly. "When are you going to be through with it?"

Ummi braved questioning looks and comments from strangers and family alike, defending against accusations of alienness that extended from our attire to our eating habits.

"What's wrong with a little pork?" Grandma and Ninie would ask at different times, in different places. "It never killed anybody."

Hardly anyone in the family understood our five pillars of faith—testimony that Allah is the one true God, prayer five times a day, supporting those in need, fasting for Ramadan, and eventually making *hajj*, the pilgrimage to Mecca—and they didn't understand why Ummi never showed her hair when outside the intimate zone of her home.

"Don't you ever think about taking that thing off your head?" Ninie would ask.

"I will when I'm ready" would be Ummi's response.

"Well, what are you waiting for?" Ninie would counter.

I don't know if Ummi had a time frame in mind, but she took her time. I imagined Ummi felt she was on the stand to regularly defend why she lived the way she lived. She could've told everyone to mind their business, but she didn't. Not even for me, as much as it might have pained her to see me endure the same kind of relentless ridicule, did I see her fight back. My impression was Ummi didn't want me to embody the Community's focus on the right to bear arms or other aggressive teachings; it was to float beyond naysayers the way we did on *jumah*. It was to be better. She continuously reminded me to ignore ignorant kids and rise above. If she could withstand the sticks and stones strangers and family members threw her way, then the bar was set for me. I was her warrior offspring, and withstanding bullies was the least I could do. But the teasing had left a mark.

When we'd first entered the Community, I was too young to know what being different felt like. Once we left, however, I felt my differentness went beyond skin color and hair texture. I didn't think people could see or understand me, unless they knew the secret codes, a word or phrase of my language, what it meant to be a Black Muslim girl in this world, to have survived sleeping on a gym mat with dozens of others whose names I didn't know.

Years later, as Ummi and I sat in her bedroom discussing the changes that took root in both of us, she admitted our reintroduction into society did not go smoothly. She confessed that while I was at school the second day, she thought about my anger from the day before, my declaration to not be Muslim.

"I was hurt, though ready to move on as well," Ummi said. "I admit, I had stopped praying yet still forced you to do so. I also knew that you were watching me, judging me."

"I was very aware of when we went from praying together to when you started watching me pray," I said. "I remember my five-times-daily *salats* turning into two: once in the morning, before I left for school, and before I went to sleep at night. I resented you made me do things that you wouldn't do."

The way Ummi remembered it, she became disinterested in the person she was from the two years before and felt the reason that woman existed at all was because of my father. She said she resented him, but also didn't put all of the blame on him.

"I missed seeing my hair as much as I missed looking into my own face," Ummi said as we sat on her bed. "It felt like every little piece of me was reawakening as I slowly remembered life before the Community. It's as if the Community, and your father, had me under a spell. While I still considered myself Muslim, I started to think, why do I have to uphold rules created for women when my husband does not uphold his end of the religious bargain?"

Ummi was told women covered their hair because, like their face and body, it was sensually divine, and the only people allowed to see us were other Muslim women, our family, or our mates. For a man, on the other hand, she understood one of the most important things he had to do was take care of his family, and she felt at that my father had failed miserably. She thought if he wasn't trying to put his best Muslim foot forward, why was she continuing to try so hard?

"Once I decided to no longer dress as a Muslim, I felt excited to walk among people the way I used to," Ummi told me that day in her bedroom. "I still believed a woman's beauty was reserved only for her mate, but if he wasn't present to receive it, why should I hide it? It was still a slow process. Harder to shed were the ideas learned from inside the Community that whistling was a call to Lucifer or that dogs were dirty pets only white people could love. Many times, my garb was my protection, a covering that separated me from others, which I liked. I also liked how quiet it made catcallers. I was ready to transition, but it was slow because I didn't know what I was doing."

When I returned home the day of my kindergarten meltdown with Red, Ummi remembered thinking I was more wrecked than she had thought I was. "Not only was your hijab off, but it had bloody splotches on it. Once I realized it wasn't your blood, I was able to process what happened to you," Ummi said. "You told me, 'He's okay, Ummi,' but I could see you weren't. If I had listened to you, that fight wouldn't have happened." Ummi looked down and closed her eyes.

"I felt I had failed you," she said, opening her eyes. "Ninie and your grandmother lobbed a lot of sticks and stones at me, but they never touched my hijab; never tried to tear it away. I was so sorry you went through that."

Seventeen

Selfish

Ummi had grown beyond three-dimensional when autumn fell in 1981. She was big, round, full-moon-size pregnant. I was curious, happy, and angry at the same time. When did this happen? At four years old, I had a book's basic understanding of how babies were made, thanks to my *Charlie Brown's 'Cyclopedia*, but Ummi never told me I was getting a sibling. As confusing was that I hadn't seen my father since we left the Community, and I had scant memories of him when we were there. I assumed if I hadn't seen my father during those times, neither had Ummi. A new baby was on the way, and while I knew the woman, the man remained a mystery to me. Neither the soon-to-be-born child nor its father were discussed with me. The world of secrets was growing wider, as though an arm reached from the Community out into our new lives with a veil so vast, I couldn't see around it.

Three weeks before the big news was finally shared with me, Ummi and Ninie cluttered the apartment with gifts for my fifth birthday. I was in the bedroom pulling off turquoise, white, purple, pink, and yellow wrapping paper that revealed various kinds of dolls. There was a beautiful Black Barbie, who blushed rouge and wore huge, cascading Diana Ross coils on her head and a white Barbie, who came with two sets of clothes. The Black Barbie was Ummi's favorite, but it was the white one, whose face was featured on the Barbie franchise house and pink Corvette box, I wanted.

In addition to the Barbies, about ten other dolls cluttered the carpeted floor, making the bedroom look like a toy factory exploded. I sat in the epicenter, surrounded by dolls of various dispositions and personalities. There were dolls that cried. Dolls that burped and repeated anything I said. Dolls that urinated and one that was a quarter of my height. I didn't know why I was given this fake nursery, but there I was, sitting on my knees, learning how each doll worked.

While I was a ball of energy, Ummi was focused on her belly. She was sitting on the edge of the queen-size bed, ruffling the forest-green quilt forward with her weight. Her feet were placed wide apart, as if to anchor her hips to the bed, and her right hand rubbed her stomach in large circular movements. Ninie sat in the living room on the sectional where she always sat, watching Ummi and me from afar with her whiskey-and-ginger-ale-on-the-rocks mix in her hand and her head, full of short black curls and white roots, cocked slightly to the left. I started to feel forgotten, ignored. My mother was tired and glowing, and it wasn't because of me. The level of concentration that zombified her into repeating the same movement, as if she were a doll wound up to repeatedly perform the same action, had nothing to do with me, and that was an irritating fact. It was at that moment when I first accepted that Ummi and her body had changed. I wondered how much I had changed.

I was celebrating my birthday, something never done in the Community, but Ummi's attention was focused elsewhere. All of a sudden, I no longer wanted to spin my brand-new, almost life-size chocolate doll around or comb another's hair, put shoes on one to take them off again. I didn't want to think about Ken and Barbie or her pink Corvette. Where were they going I couldn't go, anyway? Where was Ummi that I wasn't? Watching her hand circle obsessively, I forgot

I had just turned five, was supposed to be a big girl, and didn't always have her sitting in front of me bordered by pink ribbons and purple bows. The Community was disappearing further back in the rearview, but I still had a numb memory of Ummi's absence and believed I was owed time back from those absences.

I just turned five years old but had lived in the same home with Ummi for less than a year. I was getting used to going to school and being around other children, but I got to go back to my family and to my sanctuary every day, as the only child. I could remember in the recesses of my memory a time when I was one of dozens, when I had to share space and experiences all the time. I remembered Ummi's attention being unfocused during our *tifl* times, as it was now, and I didn't like it. I told myself I wasn't ready for whatever she was carrying or to have to share her and Ninie already. Her stomach felt like an intrusion, unwanted company, and no one asked me what I wanted, just as no one had asked me if I would have liked to move into the Community. If Ummi had asked about a baby brother or sister, I would've asked her for more time.

As I looked at Ummi sitting on the edge of the bed, her stomach looking bigger than the thirteen-inch television on the armoire, I felt movement. A spinning of the walls, sweat rolling down my temple, but Ummi didn't move. Her hand continued the same circular rhythm, and I knew my heart broke and ricocheted up to my brain, because I wasn't thinking. I could only feel. I felt myself running with feet in the air. My right foot made contact with Ummi's stomach. My closed eyes opened to the sound of her grunt as wind escaped her lips and rested squarely on my forehead. Ummi grabbed her stomach with both hands and her body pitched forward, as if she wanted to catch her ball. I saw her eyes see someone else's child when she looked at me. I didn't know what to do once my foot returned to the floor, so I started crying.

"I'm sorry, Ummi. I didn't mean to hurt you," I said.

She exhaled short bursts of breath from out-blown cheeks but still, she didn't move. She didn't look at me. Ummi knew the hardest way to hit the attention-hogger in me was to ignore it; pretend all my excess, and I, didn't exist. Make me feel like the ingrate I was. Though it was probably just a few seconds before she spoke, to me the time felt like watching an hourglass filter sand through its curves.

"You didn't hurt me," she responded, and resumed the tummy rub as if nothing happened. As if I hadn't committed the worst offense. And yet, I was disappointed for reasons I couldn't understand. Of course I didn't want Ummi hurt, but feeling replaced, like the ball in her shirt mattered more than anything else, created a new emotion for me. While Ummi was still, I could hear the plastic couch covers rustle in the living room. Ninie struggled to rise.

"What the hell you do that for!" Ninie screamed from the living room. I thought Ninie must have gotten wind of the same exhale that was still on my forehead.

"What the hell is wrong with you?" she demanded again. "You trying to hurt your mother?"

My chest tightened and my head throbbed. I didn't feel like myself. I was acting out a desire I'd been yearning to release—a selfish, angry release, like toppling a lamp or smashing dishes, just to hear the shattering sounds made as ceramics broke into smaller pieces, flying about like huge pieces of confetti. But I was the chaos, the Tasmanian devil who was giving my spot away before anyone could take it.

"You're a selfish little girl," Ninie spat. She then walked back to the green sectional, leaving me to understand without her hovering that she was right. I was selfish. My forced separation from my mother created an insecure little girl who wanted Ummi all to herself.

Eighteen

Sulaiman

I had just come home from kindergarten on a cold mid-December day when Ninie said I could finally see what Ummi had been holding in her stomach for the past nine months. I knew this meant a baby and was excited because I wanted a baby sister. Even though I had a harem of dolls that did many different things, they weren't real.

"Your grandmother's coming to pick you up. She already called," Ninie said, flicking a cigarette ash into the ashtray and some onto herself.

I dropped my book bag on the floor in the bedroom and went to the bathroom to look at myself in the mirror. I wondered if this baby would be better than me. Would everyone think she was prettier or more talented? Would she become Ninie's new favorite, and would Ninie then leave me to make *salat* alone? Fear dancing around my head aside, I was anxious about seeing my new partner in childhood. My solitary time had to wait because in less time than I thought, my grandmother rang the buzzer, walked the long corridor to our apartment, and rang the bell.

"Hello, Mrs. Hargis. How you doing?" Grandma asked Ninie. To me she said, "Come on, child, we're going to the hospital to see your mother and her brand-new baby."

Already in the car was my Aunt Love, Aunt Cookie, and my father, who was sitting behind the steering wheel. When I hopped in, he twisted around, kissed me on my cheek, and asked how I was doing.

"Are you excited?" he asked me. "I am!"

Once at New York Hospital, we rode a big metal elevator upstairs and walked past doctors and nurses dressed in pressed whites until we made it to the bright maternity ward. A short, smiling nurse with her light hair in a bun walked all of us over to a huge window where lots of small, blanketed things lay in glass cases. I looked and looked for a baby that resembled me but couldn't find one. They were white with big, bald heads. Their faces were red and their lips still quivered from the shock of breathing without their mother's help. I could tell the babies missed their mommies but didn't know how to express it.

"Do you see him?" my Aunt Love asked me in between oohs and aahs. "He's so cute," and "Oh my God, he's so handsome."

"No," I answered, unable to see past the rows and rows of scrunched, red faces.

"How don't you see him? He's the only Black baby in there," Grandma said. She pointed with her finger on the glass.

"He's right next to the baby in green," she said.

I saw her finally, the blackest and quietest baby in the room.

"He is gorgeous," my father sighed. "And he's named after a king. Sulaiman."

I admit my sibling was the most beautiful baby I'd ever seen. From the deep side part in her slicked, straight black hair to dark eyes surrounded by caramel cream and lashes extending like silken webs, I was immediately jealous but awed. The baby was an instant hit. My father kept cheesing and Grandma couldn't stop commenting on how dark he was, how much beautiful hair was on his head. Then it hit me. Everyone was calling my sister a boy. But I thought with so much hair someone had made a mistake. He should've been a girl.

Once everyone caught their breaths and breathed again, they all wanted to know how I felt—if I was happy to have a brother. Did I think he was beautiful too? How did it feel to be a big sister? I was quiet, my eyes trained on the glass, looking through at the beautiful creature. I couldn't believe how quiet he was when the other babies were crying, shaking, and driving the nurses crazy. He was as still as a statue, yet he commanded attention. When the nurses finally calmed a little one, they would walk over to my brother and stand over him. They wouldn't touch him, except to tuck the blanket tighter, but they smiled at him as if he were a rare purple-colored bird. Everyone was in love. I was ready to go home. He was cute, yes. His dark skin was beautiful, and his black eyes and hair was something to stare at. Looking at him, I felt ordinary, less talented, less pretty. He had taken my shine and wasn't even out of the little glass case yet.

Soon, the nurses said visiting hours were over. Leaving our fingerprints on the nursery's window, we walked out of the hospital into the chilled air. Everyone packed back into the car and talked, talked, talked.

"Did you see how chocolate he was?"

"Nancy's got her work cut out for her, don't she?"

"And that hair, what about that hair?"

"That baby looks Indian. He doesn't even look Black."

I sat in the back of the car, sandwiched between my two aunts, and rolled my eyes. I couldn't wait to get back to Ninie.

When he and Ummi came home several days later, she looked tired and sleepy, but her mouth wore a small smile. I could tell she had gone through a transformation. Her hair was uncombed, her skin was clean and bright, and although her stomach wasn't as big as the world she was carrying before, there was a visible little knot poking through her elastic pants. Ninie helped Ummi out of her clothes, cooed at the quiet baby, and put them both to bed. I did not think about my father, his resumed absence, or why we were not going to live together. I thought only of the baby.

Once Ummi awoke and fed him, she pulled me close and gave me a tender kiss. Calling me baby girl, she introduced me to the newest member of the family, peaceful Sulaiman. Ninie called him her Little Man, and Ummi stared at him with an alien adoration unfamiliar to me. Scooping one of my fingers into his hand, he held on and squeezed. In return I studied him, seeing what everyone else saw. Delicate features and alert, stormy eyes. Dark pink fingernails. Long black lashes. Lips the color of eggplant. We had the same parents, but I saw no resemblance between us.

"My night and day," Ummi said, as if reading my mind.

Without meaning to, Ummi was setting us apart. I wondered at her mother bear protectiveness over Sulaiman, unable to recall if she'd ever shown the same manic love to me. Whereas my infancy and babyhood felt nonexistent, simply because I couldn't remember either, I bore witness to my brother's. Ummi used the silkiest bristles to brush his hair, washed him in the gentlest of Johnson's Baby Wash, and made him smell like a baby god. His booties were handmade, crocheted by Ummi with a meditative focus, along with the *kufis* he eventually wore. Looking at this baby, I wondered if he, Abbu, and Ummi would go away in a few years and move into a big house with people who ate oatmeal and slept on mats. I questioned when he would learn Arabic and begin making *salat* or wear his first green outfit with hard brown shoes. I was curious if he would see my father as little as I did or if it would be different for him because he was a boy and new. If my father would make the family whole, as I imagined Muslim families to be, because my brother had an official Muslim name.

Months passed, and I learned my father wasn't interested in treating us differently from one another at all. He didn't call, didn't visit, and he didn't send letters or gifts. He was at the hospital after Sulaiman made his grand appearance, but after, I was never certain when I would see him. I thought if he had taken off on a fantastic voyage, Ummi should have told me. If he didn't like us, then he should have said so. I believed I would see him more because he had a boy, which the Community had taught me was the superior gender, but we didn't. While Sulaiman and I were different in many ways, neither of us were able to keep our father's love.

As winter turned to spring in 1982 and more than a year whizzed by since being out of the Community, and Ummi remained a serious Um, donning Sulaiman in the *kufis* she crocheted by hand, I felt a resentment rising that Sulaiman got to pretend to be Muslim because of his name. Unlike mine, which simply means "beautiful," the name Sulaiman is powerful. The Islamic version of Solomon. King Solomon. King Sulaiman. The warrior, Allah converter, animal whisperer. One of Allah's fiercest prophets. I would watch Ummi around him and was often annoyed at how she had turned into a swatting swan constantly protecting her young.

The three of us were heading to a store in the neighborhood one day when Sulaiman was about six months old. We passed a white couple who stopped and asked if they could see the gorgeous baby in the stroller. After an "Oh my goodness, she's gorgeous," and Ummi interrupting to say, "He's a boy," the white woman straightened up and with a huge smile on her face asked, "Is his father Indian?"

Before this, I never knew Ummi had a mean side with people. When Ninie made fun of her, she would politely ask her to stop or ignore her. Grandma would question her, sarcasm oozing, and Ummi would remain silent. Here, she put her hands on her hips, wrapped her fingers around them, and straightened her legs in her long dress. With a serious look on her face, she said, "No, he's a Black man."

The smile on the woman's face waned and the corners of her mouth got tighter and tighter until her lips almost disappeared. Still looking at the woman as if to say, *Lady, get out of the way*, Ummi peeled the ten fingers from her hips and replaced them on the stroller. Stuck, as if she had just been physically mowed over with the stroller, the woman forced another smile and replied, "I'm sorry. She is a beautiful baby."

As if hit, Ummi spun around and growled, "He's a he! He's a boy! Can't you see he's wearing blue? What's wrong with you people?"

I looked up at the woman yelling at people in the street. I didn't recognize her as the person who spoke softly, cried silently, and who once rocked me in the corner of a floor surrounded by thirty little girls and four scowling Ums. Gripping the stroller's double-curved handlebars and pushing with both hands, Ummi mumbled something about *kafirs* and how Black people make beautiful babies every day. I was quiet because I didn't remember her ever fussing over me that way. I was embarrassed. I didn't understand what made the woman's compliment offensive. When I first saw Sulaiman, I also thought he was a girl. The way Ummi kept his hair slicked on the side, I could easily see how someone would make a mistake. When we returned home, I was tired. Tired of people asking if Sulaiman was a girl, tired of people saying how beautiful he was, and tired of Ummi's anger.

When I was six and Sulaiman was one, I began to taste a little bit of the anger Ummi was always chewing on. One morning, before the sun rose, when everyone else was still rolling over, Ummi woke Sulaiman and me to hit the road.

"We're going to see your father," she said plainly.

"Where?" I asked. She didn't answer. Instead, she simply started to get us dressed in sweaters, coats, and hats.

Ummi never said where we were going, but the three of us were going to take two trains to the Greyhound bus that would drop us off at the prison grounds where my father was. With heavy lids, we shuffled to the train station with Ummi pushing Sulaiman's stroller, then to the bus depot to wait for the driver to board. While waiting, Ummi sat on the cold floor and crocheted *kufis*. We queued up behind sad, anxious women, who snacked on homemade cheese sandwiches once on the bus. When we arrived at the concrete buildings and electric gates, Ummi had completed two *kufis*, the same ones in different sizes.

I was excited to see my father but didn't like the trip. I didn't know why he was there. Walking up to the gates, barbed wire, and men dressed in uniforms that surrounded the place like a force field, I thought of the Community and the *mujahids*. The intense security reminded me of what bordered the children's playground. As within the Community, laughter, individual expressions, and visiting times were restricted. This place felt no different from the Community to me. Instead of wearing soft gray *jalabiyas*, incense, and oils, these men in power wore blue suits with buttons and big belts that held nightsticks and guns.

I didn't know why we had to walk through things that beeped and crackled, or why we were ordered to take off our jewelry, empty pockets, remove shoes, turn out socks, and wiggle our toes. While getting scanned with a handheld instrument that alarmed every time it grazed my bangled wrist, I giggled but wondered what they were looking for. Big women checked through Ummi's long dress and ran fingers over her hair, which was no longer covered by a hijab. The ritual made me think that we had done something wrong.

Once we were in front of my father and I saw his broad smile, none of the beeps, checks, or nightsticks mattered. He was happy that we were there, grinning widely, even though we were tired and Sulaiman was cranky from the journey.

"What is this place?" I asked my father. He looked at Ummi, who stared back at him expectantly.

"This place?" he asked. "Oh, it's just a place I have to stay at for a little while."

"But why? What's a little while?" I didn't understand why he would have to stay there and not with us. What made this place so important?

"It's complicated, Lala," he said, calling me by the nickname he created. "But I'll be here for a little bit. Not too long, though."

I looked around the room. The cream-colored shirt and pants he wore were identical to what the other men wore who sat leaning on their elbows over tables with their families. Everyone was in uniform. I asked him if he could leave.

"Not yet," he said.

"Is this another Community?" I asked.

My father laughed and Ummi snorted, the first sound she had made since my exchange with my father started. I looked up at her as she looked away, bending down to Sulaiman.

"You ask a lot of questions," my father said, sizing me up. "You didn't tell her, Aquila?"

"Nope," Ummi said, still not looking up.

My father put me on his knee. I was looking at him curiously, waiting to hear what no one had told me. "Is it another Community?" I asked again.

"No, this isn't another Community," my father said. "But there are rules here, just like in the Community. And just as we didn't always see each other there, it's the same thing here, until I'm able to leave. Okay? Satisfied?"

I wasn't satisfied and had plenty more questions, but I didn't ask them. I nodded and he changed the subject to school, my favorite topic.

Each time we visited thereafter, I had to mentally prepare for the trip and for seeing my father in a place that held him captive, which would make me grow a bit angrier. I told myself to be happy I got to see him at all. In the Community, I saw him less than a dozen times over two years, even though it was only the seam of Bushwick Avenue that had divided us. I remembered that he wasn't the one who greeted us when we arrived at the Community on that chilly spring day when I was two years old, and he wasn't in the car with us when Grandma drove us away when I was four. It was as if the Community had swallowed him up the moment he walked through its doors.

During that first visit, I watched as my father cooed with Sulaiman and rubbed Ummi's hand, which was stiff with self-righteousness, and I knew something wasn't right. Ummi was always uptight, and this place was soul-sucking, but she wasn't happy to see him, and she didn't pretend to be. I then understood that the trip was for Sulaiman and me, not for all of us. Ummi was offering us to my father, while also knowing we couldn't stay with him and that if we could, he wouldn't have us anyway. I soon realized my or Sulaiman's name didn't matter, nor who had been through the Community and who hadn't—our father had a different set of priorities.

I wouldn't learn the reason for my father's incarceration until I was a teenager, but even as a child I knew the Community had a gravitational pull that would continue to tsunami through our lives for years after.

PART THREE

Ashes

Nineteen

Mind Tricks

In 2018, I lost my beloved cat Allegro. We'd spent fifteen years together. Before I left the country for a two-week vacation in Portugal, Allegro was a healthy elder who knew where everything in our apartment was located. When I returned home on a Friday, I opened the door to a bony, vocal animal who was blind, emaciated, and dehydrated. By Monday, I said goodbye. An autopsy revealed brain cancer. I imagine he was sick while I was away but waited before falling apart. Maybe he didn't want to die alone. Maybe he didn't want me to return from vacation to find him dead. Whatever it was, his brain knew what to do.

I imagined my brain had worked the same way when I started remembering the Community. Like pieces of just eaten turnip, bitter but somehow sweet, I felt my brain feed the memories back to me in dreams over the years until I was able to reckon with them.

At five I was still wearing a hijab and saying prayers in Arabic. By age ten, I no longer prayed daily in any language but knew to remove my shoes when entering a house. I still said "*sapanala*" to gently wake someone, which very well could mean nothing in any language, and I still practiced Ramadan. Throughout these years, I dreamed nightly about the Community and a little girl lost, searching for her parents, without connecting that girl to myself. In middle school, anger and depression bubbled up, collided, and exploded within me. I wished for death often. I raged against Ummi and once told her I hated her. Her response was she hated me too. I didn't know why I raged but thought Ummi was to blame; maybe it had something to do with the girl who invaded my dreams every night and the threats she navigated. I felt tolerated by Ummi the way something that takes space earns attention and a sense of responsibility simply because it exists, but I didn't think Ummi took any joy in the responsibility.

A seed of inadequacy planted self-pity in me, but similar to being underwater, I was numb. To numb myself more, I would sneak a bottle of Vicks into my room and drink as much as I could before my stomach lurched. I wanted the Vicks to put me to sleep and then give a peaceful death. I experienced stomachaches and head fogs instead. By twelve, thirteen years old, I was smuggling knives from the kitchen into the bathroom and standing underneath the room's soft light with my bare feet toeing the teddy bear–brown mat below, waiting to watch my anger stain the shiny surfaces that smelled of Pine-Sol.

As much as I wanted to hurt myself, I never went deep. I couldn't actually put a name to what I felt destroyed over. I vacillated between brattiness and feeling some sense of nameless, phantom loss. During those moments of distress, I sprinkled in some therapy. It was the 1980s, and child-abuse hotline commercials were in heavy rotation on the television. I called them several times after receiving a whipping, after waiting for Ummi to leave to get cigarettes so I could hide behind the locked bathroom door and whisper to a faceless yet gentle female voice about my hurt, and I would tell her I felt suicidal. I would tell her my mother didn't love me, and I knew it because she had given me away. Each time, the gentle voice would say she was sure none of that was true. I would counter that she didn't know my mother. Then the woman would ask if I wanted someone to come over, if I wanted to press charges against my mother. I'd become indignant, afraid that

I would get Ummi into trouble, and hang up. I would then wonder if the hotlines had a log of numbers that showed up more than once and what, if anything, would happen if I called one more time. I eventually stopped.

Maybe I would've known what ached me sooner had I kept calling. Maybe it wouldn't have been years of me wrestling the Community into a double-leg takedown. Maybe I would've avoided the Vicks and the sharp blades, the taste of cherry-flavored fire and the blood that sequined alleyways on my legs to scab over and be reopened, had I known. For seven years, I think my brain hid memories of the Community out of self-protection because after I confronted Ummi in her room about them when I was fourteen years old, I didn't dream of that place again.

Twenty

My Parents—The Last Dance (late 1980s)

For years, my father was the missing person in our family portraits. When I visited Grandma in Harlem, I'd find him brewing goldenseal tea with a joint dangling between his lips as he blasted Bob Marley's "War" or Max Romeo's "Chase the Devil" from booming speakers in the back room. He was the polar opposite of my quiet, Motown-singing, hustle-dancing mother, and their differences were on full display the one time I witnessed my family try to forge a cohesive unit after years of separation.

I was twelve when my father moved into our Bushwick apartment and completed the quartet, introducing a different level of harmony for a short time. His arrival gave me, for the first time ever, the opportunity to tell a friend who called and left a message, "Oh, that was my father you spoke with." But then the tempo changed. First, my parents stopped talking. Then, they argued. Their fighting ended often with my father jumping in his green Honda and hightailing it into the darkness. When Sulaiman, who was about seven, and his best friend practiced throws and catches for upcoming games on the baseball field across the street, it was the friend's father who helped them kick up dust and who handed out high-fives while our father watched some history program six stories up on a bed. He attended one of the ten games Sulaiman played that summer. I don't remember my father attending any of my dance recitals, though Ummi was always present.

It was a dawn of a day when my parents rehearsed their final ensemble, angrily pirouetting around each other. Ummi leaped and my father caught, only to put her down and *saut de basque* away. Their volatile voices woke me.

"I can't do this anymore," Ummi said. The bass in her voice resolute.

"Fine," my father said. First calmly, then again with aggression.

To my ears, his voice had always been feathery. When debating, his hands made fluttery illustrations. I knew him as a composed man, which was how I also knew he was angry during that dance. I got up and stumbled into their concerted cacophony. To drown Ummi out, he popped a tape into the cassette player and some old soul song oozed through the speakers. He was packing, preparing to *couru* out the door to a soundtrack. I stood at the threshold of my bedroom wondering how many times I would have to watch a parent disappear.

Sulaiman awoke crying. I felt I knew what he was feeling. I imagined it felt like he was watching some part of his face disappear. When my father was done packing, he looked at us and said sorry. Ummi appeared to tower over him in her green cotton robe and white slippers. Without words, she followed him down the hallway to the door. I heard only one set of footsteps return and it was the shuffle of slippers. Devastated, Sulaiman and I fell into each other as the scent of sandalwood that my father wore lingered. I hated him and Ummi at that moment. I couldn't understand the revolving parental door. About a decade prior, I'd watched Ummi disappear across a threshold, and now Sulaiman and I watched our father disappear down a dark hallway.

The feeling of being abandoned and the desperation it brought with it returned from years before, when Ummi had disappeared through a door with me staring at the empty space she had left behind. Maybe the Community had cursed us. Maybe instead of building community, as it had promised, it had left a storm cloud over everyone instead. It seemed to have taught parents and children that they could survive without each other, trained husbands and wives to live with others. The distance created a volatile dance of anger that seemed to have been in production for years. Ummi was mumbling vigorously as she paced. "No more" was all I could hear her saying. I could tell this was Ummi's turning point with my father.

A couple of years later, around 1990 as a teenager, after sourcing my dreams with Ummi, after Sulaiman and I were over missing the musky scent of my father and debating with him to watch something other than history, Ummi said she had to tell me a story. Sulaiman was outside, riding his orange BMX bike up and down the block. Ummi was sitting on my twin-size bed in front of the wall covered with posters of Janet Jackson, Bobby Brown, and Prince. I was on the floor doing dance stretches, mentally stepping through choreography for an upcoming performance. Sinéad O'Connor's "Nothing Compares 2 U" was playing on the radio. Ummi turned it down, pushing Sinéad into the background.

"I really tried with your father, Jamiyla, but there was too much anger," Ummi said. "I gave a lot, but I also had limits."

I didn't know where she was going with this or what she wanted to say. It had been two years since my father left. I threw my legs out and pushed my chest forward. I honestly wanted to forget the two previous years had ever happened.

"But I think you need to understand something, even if you don't fully understand it now," she said. I waited. "Do you remember Um Ni'mah, a woman from the Community? One of the Ums?"

"No," I answered, intrigued. I thought about the Ums who had plagued my dreams, the Ums who took care of my group. I had only recently brought my dreams to Ummi for explanation, and now she was asking me what I remembered.

"You don't remember a woman visiting you in my place to take you outside?"

"No," I repeated. I did remember a woman who visited me and allowed me to play outside with her son, but she was inconsequential. All I thought about at that time was Ummi.

"Okay, let me ask a different question," Ummi said. "Do you remember visiting your father in prison?"

I stopped stretching and sat up straight. "Yes," I said, "I remember visiting my father in prison. I also remember no one ever explicitly saying it was prison or why he was there. I figured out it was prison on my own."

Ummi shifted on my narrow bed. "I didn't think it was my place to say. I thought your father should tell you, but I was wrong," she said, shifting again. The small bed creaked underneath her. The window was open, and the sounds of birds infiltrated her starts and stops like a score. Our tabby cat sauntered in for a quick rub and then sauntered back out of the room, leaving us to each other again.

"I hate to admit this, because I never wanted to be that mother, but your father went to prison all those years ago for killing Ni'mah's husband," Ummi said quickly, as if to close any opportunity I would have for questions. "Ni'mah would watch over you when I couldn't. She was also having an affair with your father behind my back in the Community. The affair continued after we left the Community, but I didn't know. We were at Ninie's, trying to keep it together, and that's where I focused all my energy. But he couldn't hide the affair after he killed that woman's husband, who supposedly walked in on them in the home he shared with Ni'mah, the same way someone had walked in on them years ago in the Community's closet."

Ummi took a breath and turned to the window, to the sounds of the chirping birds, to the gray pigeon that had landed on the window ledge outside. "I never wanted to be the reason for why you see your father differently. But I also want you to know who we are."

I remained silent. On the floor, I was anchored in renewed anger. Anger at my father for being despicable. Anger at Ummi for having put up with it and for just now telling me the truth behind those weary, early-morning train and bus trips, searches, and humiliations.

"I thought Ni'mah was my friend, my comrade, but she wasn't," Ummi said. "I learned they were having an affair while we were all still inside the Community. That affair followed them outside the Community and led to unexpected violence, which landed your father in prison. I can't expect him or any of the Chisholms to tell you that truth, but you should know where he was those years when we were rising before the sun warmed anything to catch a bus to a miserable place. You should know why I was so evil."

Ummi stood up, treelike over me, her knees creaking, then she squatted. She kissed me on the cheek and looked me in the eyes. Neither of us said anything. My legs were still splayed out in a straddle stretch on the floor. Ummi was still squatting. I broke the silence.

"I'm sorry, Ummi, that sounds devastating," I said. I closed my legs. "I have no idea why you didn't leave him then."

"I don't know why either," she said, standing up. "I didn't want to ruin you and Sulaiman before you had to be or to be the cause of it." I stood up and hugged her. Sadness washed over me. I couldn't imagine what she felt, with two young children, traveling to visit a husband who had betrayed all of us in such a scandalous way.

"If you can believe it," Ummi said, "at the time, before I knew the truth, I stood behind him. I believed then that the only reason a Black man would be sent to prison was because the government had conspired against him. And coming from the Community, that did not feel like a conspiracy theory." Ummi paused. I was now sitting on the bed next to her, looking down at my bare feet, at my hands, at my glitter nail polish.

I appreciated the candor, the truth, but was admittedly dumbfounded by her blind faith, her willingness to compartmentalize. I was only a teenager but didn't think I could believe in a place that mandated the breaking up of families, that gave one person most of the power. I didn't think I would be able to trust a person, like my father, who wanted to make the Community his community, who was okay not seeing his wife and child. I marveled at how naive Ummi sounded to me and how naive she must have been to have said yes, to my father, to the Community, to leaving her old life behind for the sake of keeping her family together in some way. Dwight York obviously preyed on people like my parents, who desperately sought and hoped for change and self-empowerment, even if that meant sacrificing pieces of their core beliefs.

"We were constantly told that we were being watched. That when a Brother had been arrested, it was because he was a soldier. It was because the Man didn't want us to thrive," Ummi said. "It was also because we might have had an informant in-house, that Big Brother was always watching Black people and always trying to take down leaders who taught us self-empowerment, that I told myself part of the reason your father was in prison was because the system was unjust."

"Really?" I asked, in a tone that bordered on accusatory.

"Yes, really, because I had seen it happen in my own lifetime. Remember, I was a girl when Medgar, Malcolm, Martin, and then Fred was killed. Fred Hampton was only twenty-one when Chicago police put a bullet in his head; I was twelve. I was about nine when Muhammad Ali said no to the Vietnam draft and was fined and sent to jail instead. And even though Granny never spoke about it, all of it was big news back then. So, I knew what the government did to Black men, and I believed they wanted to do the same with the Community."

Ummi looked toward the open window again, as if it could transport her back a decade. "No one can tell me that we weren't under surveillance," she said, turning to me. "Partly because there were shady things going on inside, like guns and welfare fraud, but mainly because we were Black and Muslim. So, coming up against law enforcement was not a surprise to me. Having to kill a person was not a surprise to me. The surprise was that your father had killed another Black man, and that Black man was Ni'mah's husband. I sacrificed my freedom, joined the Community, to keep our family together. Your father gave up his freedom for something that had nothing to do with liberation."

Twenty-One

September 11, 2001

I was in my early twenties, working for a small independent television network down the block from the United Nations. The sky was crystal clear. Not a cloud hovered. I had an off-site screening and was running late into the office. I remember praying if I could get in the building no later than 9:05 a.m. it would be a good day. Underground was crowded with straphangers heading to work. Aboveground wasn't so crowded, and I felt the lilt as soon as I exited Grand Central and crossed a quiet Lexington Avenue. People seemed to move in slow motion on the sidewalks. On Third Avenue, traffic wasn't humming, taxis weren't honking or swerving, and morning dog walkers weren't out for the first day's pee.

I heard two motionless people mention "plane." The word itself wasn't ominous. During college, I lived in Rochdale Village in Jamaica, Queens, a residential complex situated so close to JFK airport that we endured the incessant whiz of low-flying jets the way people who live near subway lines endure the slight tremors of passing trains. Sometimes when a plane flew by the building, it felt like the nose might crash into our sixth-floor window, or that a wing would snap off the corner of the building, which it never did. The high school I graduated from is an aviation school. The campus proudly housed an aircraft on the grounds, as an homage to the school's namesake and Tuskegee airman August Martin. Nothing about the word "plane" should have given me pause, but it did at that moment. Maybe it was that people looked worried or that it was rush hour and no one was rushing. Maybe it was the half-desolate avenue.

Once I hit Second Avenue, I felt the kinetic shift; New York City was missing its normal vehicular traffic. There were no yellow taxis, no black Hummers, no silver Lexus. Instead, blue-and-white police cars and siren-red fire trucks ripped through the streets' silence. People were standing in the middle of the avenue, eyes strained downtown. I kept moving because I was almost at the exterior of my office building, almost not late. I saw my friend and colleague Christina running toward me from First Avenue. Her face beet-colored and twisted in fear. Her eyes big and her mouth wide as if trying to scream. Her long dark hair was streaming behind her as she ran. I thought something horrible had happened to her. When she reached me, she grabbed me by my arm.

"We're under attack! We're under attack!" She screamed those three words repeatedly as she pulled me into the elevator bank and frantically pressed the number two button. She was sweating and breathing so heavily she couldn't catch her breath.

"What are you talking about, 'we're under attack'?" I asked with a hint of humor. "I have a screening today I'm trying not to be late for."

We got to her floor and she pulled me off the elevator. Christina pointed with her free hand to the huge flat-screen television on the wall in front of us.

"Look!" she said.

The shaky news camera showed one of the Twin Towers engulfed in black smoke and a plane's tail dangling from its side like a misdirected shark gone airborne. Hordes of people were screaming, and the voice on the television was saying another plane was approaching. I looked around the room to see who was watching, to make sure I wasn't hallucinating, and I saw my boss, other coworkers, and clients watching the television with anguished faces. The room was devoid of sound except for the voices coming from the flat-screen on the wall. Christina still clutched my arm.

Like the shark in *Jaws* appearing as a dark underwater mass, a huge shadow floated into the frame. Another plane piloted toward the second tower's eightieth floor. My heart stopped, dropped, and shot right up into my air passage. The news reporter kept repeating, "We're under attack! America is under attack!"

"See!" Christina said. She had the eyes of a woman afraid of what's in the forest.

I saw but I couldn't believe. I saw the smoke and I saw the plane and I felt my arm raise my hand to my mouth, but I couldn't believe. I heard the reporter repeatedly yell, "America is under attack!" He might as well have been speaking Swahili—I couldn't understand.

My mind went back to winter 1993 when I was a junior in high school and working on Broadway not too far from the World Trade Center. I remember being on the last A train that made it out of Fulton Street station before a massive bomb exploded and shook the entire area so fiercely, we first thought it was an earthquake. Six people died. I remember shaking my head when the self-professed bomb master Ramzi Yousef bragged he hoped to kill 250,000 people. It was a fiery try without fireworks. As horrible as the incident was, New Yorkers didn't fathom losing twin landmarks. We loved our buildings more than we loved seeing the sky, and everyone had a soft spot for New York City at the end of the day. "I Love New York" isn't a slogan as much as it is a mantra. Yet what I witnessed eight years later was much worse than what I saw in 1993.

Once the talk of traveling ash, debris, and smoke started, it was like I had snapped out of a stupor. Ummi was attending classes at the Borough of Manhattan Community College, a school within walking distance of the Towers, and she worked in the West Village, two miles from the World Trade Center, which felt close at the time. She could have been at either place, and they were both too close to the scene for my comfort. The newscaster said that all of downtown Manhattan was covered in white soot.

Right when I was about to put one foot in front of the other to run upstairs to my office and call her, my periphery caught suits hurling into the air from the gaping holes of one building, one after another, like soaring penguins leaping off an iceberg. Then the giant mass of metal and glass buckled and collapsed under its own destroyed weight. I'm sure there was sound on the television when that happened, but I heard nothing; the close sound of my breath drowned out everything else. I was sweating through my blouse and suit jacket.

I said, "Oh my God," both hands covering my mouth. I remember running, tripping up the wood stairs to the third floor, and into my office. I was terrified. Every piece of me that had tried to give humanity the benefit of the doubt went out the window with the jumpers. The world was mad. Neither my office phone nor any of my coworkers' worked. My cell phone wouldn't call out. I frantically turned the television on in my office and listened as the words "Islamic terrorists," "jihad," and "war" boomed from the tiny speakers and electrified the air around me. Sick about what was to come, how close I was to the UN, and how close my mother was to death and chaos, I replaced my pumps for flip-flops, preparing myself to walk more than forty city blocks downtown to Ummi. Anyone who had anyone in or near the Financial District was having conniptions. People with family members who worked in the Towers were already foot-racing downtown.

I returned to the second floor for Christina, who was making calls and working her schedule as though New York hadn't stepped into a DC Comics story. I snatched the phone from her, hung up on whoever was on the line, and half dragged her toward the elevator doors. Back outside, we walked past pay phone after pay phone, calculating which had the shortest lines and if it was worth waiting on one or best to keep moving forward. We walked past phone booths with people bawling, their heads banging against the interior partition, and pay phones with a disgruntled line of people who were upset that a person with a seemingly infinite coin purse of quarters would use them all and not share.

When I finally got to a pay phone with a short line and spoke with Ummi, she said she and everyone else were in the bomb shelter of her office building. I wasn't sure why an administrative nursing home building for the elderly and HIV patients needed a bomb shelter, but I imagined they needed it for when HIV/AIDS care wasn't so popular. I breathed a little easier knowing she was sheltered, but I was in a war zone. As Christina and I quick-stepped our way down Second Avenue—from Forty-Second to Thirty-Fourth to Fourteenth Street—we encountered dozens of people awash in white dust. Some were holding bleeding heads; others had big red blotches splashed across their white button-downs. Those who escaped looked like they had either been introduced to evil by the devil or were walking dead. My heart bled for those dazed souls, and as much as I wanted to stop, give their parched, blanched lips sips of the water I was carrying, I couldn't stop. I had been flip-flopping my way downtown for an hour and wasn't far from Ummi. Christina and I split in the Village when I veered west and she continued home to Chinatown.

I was crossing Seventh Avenue, via Christopher Street, moving in the direction of the pier, when I spotted a young woman wearing a hijab. She was standing on the sidewalk hugging her petite frame. Across the street stood a row of men yelling "terrorist bitch" and "we should kill you for what your people did." She was shaking and turning slowly in circles. Without thinking, I took her arm and started walking away from the men. She was wearing a black backpack, blue jeans, and hard black shoes. She clutched a textbook to her chest. I asked her name and where she lived. I've forgotten her name, but she said she lived in New Jersey; her family lived in Pakistan. She was alone in the country, attending college. She said she had tried but couldn't reach her roommate. It was impossible to walk away from her.

I told her I was going to my mother and we might be able to help her, give her shelter and a plan to get home. I promised I would help. She didn't instantly trust me, and I understood that as well. She was probably more terrified than I was.

As we approached Ummi's office building, I saw her propped in the doorway, peeking out with an odd expression on her face. I think I was smiling; I was so happy to see her. I asked the girl to wait while I spoke with my mother and quickly told Ummi how I found the girl.

"We've got to help her," I said to Ummi. I thought if anyone understood the desperation I felt to make sure this young woman wasn't hurt through no fault of her own, it would be my mother.

Ummi looked me in the eyes and asked, "What makes you think we have to help her?" Then, "You can't bring her."

"But she has no family! She has no place to go, no one to help her. We have to help her," I repeated.

"You don't know this girl. You pick her up off the street and it's a war out here. You don't know her." Sneaking a quick look at the young woman, Ummi asked, "And what's in her backpack anyway?"

I could not believe my mother, my Ummi, was judging another Muslim woman because of her appearance. While I didn't know all the facts that led to those nightmare events in New York, Pennsylvania, and Washington, nor equated "terrorist" with "Muslim," I knew there was a long history of contention between the Middle East and the United States. Nonetheless, I strongly believed the young woman I dragged from a potential mob wasn't responsible for the buildings falling. Living here, breathing the same air we did, she was a victim like the rest of us, and I was baffled that Ummi disagreed.

"What's in her backpack, Jamiyla?" Ummi asked again.

"Books, Ummi, books! She's a student. Students carry books in backpacks. And if she had a bomb, she would've exploded when those men were threatening her."

"Well, she still can't come in," Ummi said. Resolved. Her lips pinched together, signaling her stance.

"Are you serious? Tell me you're not serious."

I felt Ummi was senseless with the shock of someone who'd witnessed towers crumble and white powder overcome streets for miles. I wanted any explanation except one that led me to think she was an ignorant, racist American. Ummi was unwavering.

"Yes, I'm serious," she said. "Security is tight, and they're only letting you in because you're my daughter. I'm sorry, Jamiyla, but we're at war and she can't come in." Holding my chin in one hand, she leaned in and said, "You can't save everyone."

A burst of angry tears fell—hot tears I'd been holding back since witnessing the fall of the North and South Towers. I wanted to turn around, in a graceful pivot, and walk away. I wanted to grab the student by the arm and hike across a bridge to my apartment in Brooklyn. I wanted to scream "Traitor!" at Ummi. It was as if she didn't know who I was. Or that she had created something she was too afraid to honor. She was Dr. Frankenstein and I was the Monster. The experiment. I wanted to ask if she was aware of all I had sacrificed? I felt Ummi had confessed to a lie that day but only because she didn't think there would be a tomorrow. How she stood there stolidly saying she suspected a lone Muslim student to be a terrorist was something I couldn't comprehend or forget. I was incensed by what I perceived as weak betrayal. Long before I read Ummi's letter about her childhood, she had told me she felt she could never tell my father no to moving into the Community because she knew he would join without us and continue to move through the world as if he weren't a married father, just as he told her he would in 1978. Yet I had moved through a crumbling Manhattan to be with her and was pissed at how easily she said no to me.

Right when the United States' Godzilla was knocking down building after building and innocent Muslims in the city were being targeted, my inner struggle and my struggle against Ummi placed me at an emotional crossroads on 9/11. The word "American" was taking on new meaning for me when it already had so many different connotations depending on which side of the line one stood. Choices, democracy, freedom, rights, or capricious, imperialistic, violent, xenophobic. As an American, I was taught that I could do anything. I had witnessed my family become Muslim, then not. We had braced against ridicule and signed ourselves up to be ostracized, because that was our right to do so, in so proving we could be anything we wanted. We had walked around hidden from others, only to hide now behind a country we once turned our backs on because it had turned its back on us. To my surprise, Ummi was shameless in turning her back on this student.

Still crying, I walked back to the girl and told her security wouldn't let her in. I said I was sorry.

"I understand," she said. "I thank you for all you've already done." She then turned east and crossed the street. When I walked back to Ummi, whose arms were wide open as if all I needed to quell my anger was a strong maternal embrace, I couldn't look at her. I was seething. Was this the same woman who had carried me into a communal mosque as a small child and who once believed in the unification of all Muslims?

Ummi seemed genuinely confused by my being upset. Unbeknownst to her, her behavior exploded the sleeping TNT burrowed in my chest for the past two decades. It took a foreign, helpless young Muslim woman, hidden even from those who should have understood her, for me to realize I was a stranger to Ummi. When I tried to address the incident months later, Ummi used silence as her method of protest. When I broached it years later to finally unearth where she was mentally all those years ago, she said she didn't remember. And I didn't believe her; how could anyone forget anything that happened that day?

It took me many years later to see the incident through a different lens. What if Ummi was sincerely afraid, as we all were, of the destruction happening in New York City and could only think of making sure

I survived? Maybe this was a maternal instinct that left no space for anyone other than her child. Could it be those years separated in the Community left a wound so deep she could never chance splitting her attention or unwittingly putting me in harm's way by doing something she thought was good and just? Was that her way of trying to make sure she didn't make the same mistake twice? I will never forget that Muslim student—who reminded me of the uncertainty and loneliness I had felt inside the Community, as well as during the first days of kindergarten—the crashing of the World Trade Center, or even the way Ummi's face crumbled when she saw me with the young woman. At twenty-four years old, and no one's parent, I identified with the student. I put myself in her hard black shoes and found it almost impossible to imagine being away from my family as my host country was reporting a war against people who looked and prayed like me. I was genuinely afraid for her. Desperation can make people do desperate things.

Twenty-Two

Ground Zero (One Week Later)

The growing wedge between Ummi and me was becoming a chasm. Where I averted my eyes from newspapers with the word "jihad" as a selling point, Ummi would exhale relief that we were not in the "crazy" house, as she said, when the buildings fell. "Can you imagine if we were in the Community now?" she asked. In our T-shirts and jeans, uncovered heads and faces, we avoided any accusations of not being patriotic. The country had a new group under the microscope. Three days after my city lost its directional compass, I felt so ambivalent about Ummi I lost the words to speak to her.

Rather than brood over my fractured mother-daughter relationship, Christina and I took to the streets with a still camera and a tape recorder seven days after the attacks. Christina was taking photography classes, and as a new journalist, I was interested in archiving New York's collective emotions. People were either intuiting or disregarding their neighbors' needs, and the heartbreak of 9/11 continued to play out on repeat the week after. Only one news channel dominated, reporting smolder, vanished souls, and the continual destruction of buildings that once stood near the Twin Towers. When friends and families of World Trade Center employees and first responders weren't pleading into the cameras for information or a location on their lost ones, "Terrorist Attack!," "Muslims," and "Jihad!" were inescapable words heard on the television and seen in newspaper headlines. Cave-made videos of a tall, lanky man named Osama bin Laden were discovered, and the image of bearded, tanned men in white turbans with big black machine guns hoisted on shoulders who claimed responsibility for toppling New York City introduced me to a new, deadlier gang called al-Qaeda. The country braced itself and all but declared anyone who shared the same skin tone as those monsters a pariah.

In seven days, the World Trade Center became Ground Zero, and this deficit altered even the air. With the rest of the country, I became obsessed with the news, vacillating between depression and disgust as I took in the aftershocks of the attacks, the massive loss of innocent lives, and the desperation felt from the victims' loved ones. One minute I was hopelessly in tears and the next I was angry, plotting a way out of the country, carrying my passport around in case I had to abruptly jet. I couldn't shake the image of people jumping out of windows or of bloody, ashen faces drifting up Second Avenue. I was fearful. I felt helpless. I wanted old New York City back, with its kind halal food truck and coffee cart vendors, being forced to wait while they completed their prayer and hurriedly, yet lovingly, folded up a prayer rug to resume business and thank people for their patience. I wanted the New York City back that wasn't threatened by someone who had to make *salat* before handing over a buttered bagel.

The country was permeated with distrust, fear, and pain, so Christina and I went searching for answers to this hurt. We each had black bandannas tied around our faces to block out the heavy air. We approached two young women: one pale and blonde, the other brown with jet-black hair. The cinnamon girl's pretty face was taut with caution. I pulled down the bandanna and explained Christina and I were in the smog with a camera and tape recorder because we were concerned Americans were terrorizing brown people for looking like terrorists. I asked if she had encountered any racism since the plane attacks. She looked offended.

"I'm not Muslim. I'm Indian, South Asian. So, no," she said. Her mouth clamped back together and locked in any additional thoughts I hoped to get from her. Annoyed, the two friends then pushed past Christina and me.

What I learned from the young Indian woman was what I had learned from Ummi several days prior—it was better to be anything than Muslim right now. I was stunned at how quickly the word had become a curse, like saying "Voldemort" in Harry Potter's world. Overnight, Muslims became the "you know who" or the people who "must not be named." They became a different version of Ralph Ellison's Invisible Man, who confirmed, "I am invisible, understand, simply because people refuse to see me." I knew this united feeling of fear, the perception of being a threat, as a Black woman. I remembered that feeling after we had left the Community and I was still wearing a hijab. I ached knowing this was how Muslims were feeling and doubly ached if they were Black Muslims or born elsewhere. How much societal angst could one person endure?

Christina and I discussed the Indian woman's words and headed down Second Avenue, periodically pausing to say prayers for people we never knew but who were now immortalized in pictures posted on placards and posters. Then we were stopped in our tracks, as if by a force of anger. We were in the East Village, somewhere around First Avenue, when we spotted an angry mob in the street screaming and pumping white banners with red-and-black letters into the night air. There were some women, but the crowd consisted mainly of white and Black men. They were shouting "Terrorists!" and "Go back where you came from!" Some yelled, "We should kill you!"

With camera and tape recorder in hands, Christina and I turned to the mob. To our left was the shattered storefront of an Egyptian restaurant. The cracks in the glass spread like splayed fingers. The restaurant's employees were as far away from the door as physically possible. Looking into the restaurant, we could see them huddled together in the back. Oddly, there were no police or news cameras present. Christina and I wondered if the police had been called and just didn't show. Was all of New York City's law enforcement trying to save the buried? Or did these Egyptians think calling the cops was as scary as facing a mob of angry men? Christina and I left the scene, too shaken to engage anyone.

As we walked away, we agreed that this was exactly where African Americans had been for at least a hundred years, post-Emancipation, and where Chinese Americans were in 1871 after a mob in Los Angeles murdered more than a dozen people. Christina, whose Chinese family had emigrated from Tanzania, noted that she wouldn't have been there on Second Avenue with me had the Chinese Exclusion Act of 1882 not been repealed. Our ancestors had walked different paths in this country, but we both knew they had faced fear head-on, stared down terrorists, and refused to leave a shop simply because a brick or crowbar had been launched through the window. We knew why many would hesitate to notify authorities for fear the authorities might prove to be more menace than refuge. The feeling that one suffers alone but also as a collective, the belief that someone else's situation is worse, and there's no need harping over a busted window when someone else could as easily be crying over a busted head, eye, nose, face. Racism was such a powerful concept, we thought, that people who lacked power often hesitated to see themselves as victims. Instead, they think if they hadn't been there, this wouldn't have happened. If they hadn't made eye contact, they might not have been noticed. If they hadn't been Black or Muslim or a woman or gay, they would be safe.

I understood this fear as if by osmosis from old news footage, films, and stories told by my elders who grew up in the South or in Harlem. "The police are the last people we call for help," Grandma would say to my cousins and me. I grew up on hip-hop, a culture that made chart-topping records about crooked cops and police brutality. Consequently, I imagined the lack of police presence at the Egyptian restaurant stemmed from fear. I also knew well the flip side of fear and the hate it could spawn because of how I had first feared, then hated the freckle-faced kid in my kindergarten class who teased me for being

Muslim. I didn't know those men cowering in the restaurant, the same way I didn't know the random Muslim student a week prior, but I knew what it felt like to be an outcast, to be called afraid.

When I got home and stood in my own solitude with the past few days on rotation in my head, I wondered where the country would go from here. Could we heal? What would it take for us to remember our humanity? Would I ever see the two things that raised me, Ummi and New York City, the same again? Could I release the image of Ummi and I having selective memory soldiers that moved around each other like pieces on a chessboard, evading, to sometimes square off? I felt Ummi and I were experiencing our own Ground Zero. We were a destructive duo brimming with ego, emotions, and years of anger. I thought her hypocritical and selfish. I hated that she wouldn't apologize for the Community. On the other hand, she saw me as pretentious and condescending, a curmudgeon who just wanted to be angry.

My anger imploded on September 20, when then president George W. Bush stood in the House Chamber and declared war, for national security purposes, he said, against Afghanistan, al-Qaeda, and the Taliban. War? Wasn't Desert Storm launched not so long ago under the other Bush? I sat in my living room as the announcement played on C-SPAN, my mouth open.

"The only way to be safe is to publicly pledge allegiance to that flag," I said out loud to no one. I remembered when Ummi had taught me never to say the pledge, and the excuse for abstaining was for my religion. I wondered if then were now, would Ummi still have encouraged Isa's teachings, or would she have distanced herself from Islam the way she had distanced herself from the student last week? As a child, I wanted so badly to create distance between the Community and me, to narrow my reach to Ummi, and now, at twenty-four, I wanted distance from everything—from the Community, Ummi, and the US.

Epilogue

Three years after 9/11, I moved to Japan. Hiroshima became my new Ground Zero. Living overseas in a country where I often receded into silence felt ironically more comforting than being in the United States, where I increasingly felt like an outsider and spoke with rage. Being in Hiroshima, an immigrant, forced me to reflect, to slow down. I thought about the Community—that my parents had once believed in a man who was now serving a 135-year sentence for child abuse—and it was hard to make nice. The sixteen-hour difference and vast Pacific Ocean that separated Hiroshima from New York City salved my conscience. I easily made new friends and laid claim to a new life.

When I returned to the States a little over a year later to work with a volunteer group in New Orleans after Hurricane Katrina, a new attitude arose between Ummi and me. For years, I hadn't remembered there ever was a source for the raging anger I felt. I only knew that once the memory was revealed and confirmed on the day I ran into my mother's room for an explanation about a recurring dream, a fuse had been lit and a dormant bomb exploded. Toiling in New Orleans among strangers and Ummi's eventual apology helped me release the heart-heavy, muddled emotions I carried about the Community. I hadn't known an apology was the catalyst I needed to heal until it was offered. Only then was I able to forgive Ummi.

She and I worked to be nice to one another and, even more so, honest. Yet when I think about the exact moment that propelled Ummi and me toward each other again, I can't name it. I know it was filled with tears, denials, and a stream of apologies. The monotone buzzing of a dial tone was often heard by both of us as we lost patience, lost words, hung up; then we'd take breaths, maybe call a friend to vent, and ring the other back to make amends. Ummi would say she loved me. She would say, *I'm sorry*. I would say, *I'm sorry too*, because I wasn't the only one who suffered as a result of some ground zero from some incomprehensible moment in our lives. Ummi said she genuinely thought that she was doing a good thing when she joined the Community. I believed her. What sane parent would willingly put their child in harm's way?

I still think about the ramifications of the Community, or any similar idea, has on people. I remember a day when I was about fourteen or fifteen years old and heard Ummi scream from her bedroom. When I got to her, I found her standing in front of the television with her hand to her mouth, eyes wide. She motioned me closer. Motioned for me to look at the screen. The newscaster was reporting on a mother who had jumped out a window with her daughter in her arms. Both died.

"I knew her," Ummi said.

The camera panned to devastated family members.

"We knew her," Ummi said.

"We?" I asked.

"Yes. In the Community. She was in the Community with us. What did that place do to her?"

I remember staring at Ummi, wondering if that could have ever been us. I wondered if Ummi had ever thought about cajoling Sulaiman and me out onto the fire escape, scooping us up in each of her arms to tilt forward, and allowing gravity and ground to do what they do. Ummi's question—What did that place do to her?—was a question of who gets to survive and who doesn't. Who goes batshit crazy following a stint of isolation, hunger, having a child taken from them, and who is able to stuff those experiences into an emotional suitcase that lives on the very top shelf in a closet and move on? At that time, with Ummi gripping my hand in front of the television, I thought it proved that we were resilient, as well as damaged.

In addition to the woman who flew out her window, I wondered how many families who didn't make the news crashed and crumbled because they looked for love or identity in the wrong places. Because they felt so emasculated and dejected by society that the only way to freedom was to voluntarily isolate. I wondered if a Dwight York or a Jim Jones would have existed and amassed a following had the citizens of this country felt like citizens who could expect justice and respect.

Cultural vulnerability, when up against powerful arms of society that control all resources and ultimately livelihoods, have led many to seek their own forms of liberty in the people and places who appear to share their vision even when they don't. There are days when I find it difficult to completely blame York for stealing souls when those souls, for the most part, willingly went with him. It was the child abuse, physical for me and sexual for others, that I cannot comprehend. The rumor of how parents would offer their young for crumbs was too reminiscent of slavery. Who protects children if not their parents?

On the other hand, York's predatory ways, his schemes to rob families and lord over lives, was such a classic case of narcissistic-psychopathic crazy that I find it difficult to believe no one saw it. Today, anyone can type Dwight York's name into a search engine and view more sites and chats devoted to debunking lies and conspiracies stacked against him than not. He remains a god, even while in prison for the rest of his life.

Knowing what I know now of my mom's childhood and my father's early political leanings, it's almost impossible for me to stay angry with them because of the Community. Considering their youth and personal experiences, the historical circumstances that continue to play out today with law enforcement in the immortalized names of Sandra Bland,

Tamir Rice, George Floyd, and so many others, I can understand why they were attracted to York and his branded message of Islam. York told them they were beautiful, intelligent, worldly people who didn't have to put up with being second-class citizens. He showed them power. He told them they didn't have to stay in a country that abused and lied to them; they could go to Africa, to Sudan specifically, and be free.

After the Black Lives Matter movement launched in 2013, with the acquittal of Trayvon Martin's killer, and grew into the largest civil rights movement since the 1960s, parallels emerged between the way 1960s Black organizations were infiltrated and dismantled, how Muslim men were treated during the War on Terror for their religion, and how BLM activists and protesters were targeted during the Trump administration. With each group, the government claimed they surveilled them for security purposes. Against each group, law enforcement used brute force, false charges, and false narratives. In 2015, NYPD commissioner Bill Bratton practically compared BLM protesters to a terrorist group by stating that their activism had to be handled similarly to how the perpetrators of the horrific violence that took place in Mumbai in 2008 and in Paris in 2015 were handled.

People who have been trampled upon, robbed, and vampired of their traditions, and then told for centuries that their lives matter none, may eventually resist oppression like their lives depend on it. Others might find themselves at an identity crossroads, if wearing two faces, as W. E. B. Du Bois wrote, becomes unbearable. When that happens, desperation can set in. Some might join a crew, a gang, an organization to stamp out such desperation and reclaim a concentrated power by using sentimentality. The sentimentality could be about the good old days, how to rebirth, or how to become masters of their own destinies. When seeking in despair, one can miss sentimentality as the pitch or mishear the person who claims to have the keys to freedom.

James Baldwin wrote about sentimentality's disingenuousness in the 1949 essay "Everybody's Protest Novel," aptly comparing sentimentality to dishonesty. The way to steer clear of this dishonesty is to address the nation's deep wounds of racism, patriarchy, and white supremacy rather than poking at them. Sentimentality can explain how people who felt left behind by a changing nation fervently voted for a president who bashed anyone on the margins and promoted a return to the before times. It can explain why families still believed that if they braved the elements with their children and made it to the US border, they would not have their children taken from them, because no one could have imagined such a thing would be a national policy in a country that once sang of its immigrant roots. And sentimentality can explain some of the events that led up to the insurrection at the Capitol in Washington, DC, on January 6, 2021, as well as why the white mob was handled so gingerly. I could see the parallels of all these instances in the experiences of my own family, and it was sentimentality, I believe, that my parents also fell for.

Once I forgave Ummi for the Community, I could look at how it shaped and soldered me. I could step away and size it up from an arm's length. From today's contentious cultural climate around Black lives, the police, Muslims, migrants, and everyone else, the Community, in all its conservative and extreme leanings, was essentially saying to anyone with eyes that Black lives mattered. The Community was my parents' way of echoing and indoctrinating this knowledge into my cells early, before I quickly learned from others and believed that my life didn't matter. I understand my parents were molded by a world full of extremes and that they felt the way to surf it was to counterbalance with an extreme of their own. I believe to my core they thought the Community would save us.

I remember my Ummi saying once during a conversation about the Community, "My lack of understanding shouldn't get in the way of me experiencing love." She was right. They may not have known what they were getting into, but I am thankful my parents had the foresight to know it was important that I learned and believed in love, on a cellular level, early on.

ACKNOWLEDGMENTS

It was with the extreme compassion, patience, and love of my mother, Nancy Hamilton, that I was able to tell this story. I am forever grateful for her courage, her grace, and for her encouraging my love of words—from the constant purchasing of books when I was a child to reading my short stories and really bad poetry. I love you, Ummi. Sulaiman Chisholm, brother, your patience is a study in compassion. I am thankful to my grandmothers, Dorothy "Ninie" Hargis and Dorothy "Grandma" Johnson, and to the Chisholms for allowing me to be me.

To Jeanine Costley, PhD, my sister, for the loving words, the emotional prop-ups, endless calls, and for your unwavering support that this story mattered.

To my Writing Tribe—Ayana Byrd, Rita Hickey, Sue Jaye Johnson, Karen Good Marable, and Kenrya Rankin—thank you for the text check-ins, writers' retreats, chapter reads, advice and wisdom, ears for venting, arms for pushing, words of encouragement and support, and for every observation shared.

To my alma maters: the City College of New York for igniting the first ember in me, as an insecure undergrad, that I had a story to tell; the University of Southern California for inspiring me to think deeper about children and learning differences; and to the Writer's Foundry at St. Joseph's College, where I received my MFA, for the countless writing workshops, revisions, and community. Thank you to Justin Torres for encouraging me to continue writing; you were inspiring.

To my agent, Claudia Cross of Folio Literary Management, for believing in this book.

To the writing collective in New York City, Paragraph, for making it so that Claudia and I crossed paths.

To Amazon's Little A for saying yes.

To everyone at Little A who worked on this book, including editors Laura Van der Veer, Carmen Johnson, and Mosi Secret.

To El-Hajj Malik El-Shabazz, Ntozake Shange, James Baldwin, and Toni Morrison for inspiring me to think critically about power and oppression.

ABOUT THE AUTHOR

Photo © 2021 Sue Jaye Johnson

N. Jamiyla Chisholm was born in New York City and grew up in Brooklyn. She graduated from City College in New York City, received her master of arts in teaching from the University of Southern California, and received her MFA from the Writer's Foundry at St. Joseph's College in Brooklyn. As a journalist, Jamiyla has written countless articles focused on culture, race, and women, and she has worked with numerous media companies and publications, including COLORLINES, *Essence*, TIME'S UP, *VIBE*, and *The Source*. Jamiyla is an avid traveler, runner, and language learner. She lives in Brooklyn with her cat Reesies.